PRESIDENTS CONFRONT REALITY

From Edifice Complex to University Without Walls

A REPORT FOR THE CARNEGIE COUNCIL
ON POLICY STUDIES IN HIGHER EDUCATION

Lyman A. Glenny, John R. Shea

Janet H. Ruyle, Kathryn H. Freschi

PRESIDENTS
CONFRONT
REALITY

*From Edifice Complex
to University Without Walls*

Jossey-Bass Publishers
San Francisco · Washington · London · 1976

PRESIDENTS CONFRONT REALITY
From Edifice Complex to University Without Walls
　　　by Lyman A. Glenny, John R. Shea, Janet H. Ruyle, Kathryn H. Freschi

Copyright ©1976 by:　The Carnegie Foundation
　　　　　　　　　　　for the Advancement of Teaching

　　　　　　　　　　　Jossey-Bass, Inc., Publishers
　　　　　　　　　　　615 Montgomery Street
　　　　　　　　　　　San Francisco, California 94111

　　　　　　　　　　　Jossey-Bass Limited
　　　　　　　　　　　3 Henrietta Street
　　　　　　　　　　　London WC2E 8LU

*The Carnegie Council on Policy Studies in Higher Education,
2150 Shattuck Avenue, Berkeley, California 94704, has sponsored
preparation of this report as part of a continuing effort to
obtain and present significant information for public discussion.
The views expressed are those of the authors.*

*Copies are available from Jossey-Bass, San Francisco,
for the United States, Canada, and Possessions.
Copies for the rest of the world are available from
Jossey-Bass, London.*

Library of Congress Catalogue Card Number LC 75-24014

International Standard Book Number ISBN 0-87589-272-8

Manufactured in the United States of America

DESIGN BY WILLI BAUM

FIRST EDITION

Code 7523

The Carnegie Council Series

The Federal Role in Postsecondary
Education: Unfinished Business,
1975-1980
*The Carnegie Council on Policy
Studies in Higher Education*

Low or No Tuition: The Feasibil-
ity of a National Policy for the
First Two Years of College
*The Carnegie Council on Policy
Studies in Higher Education*

More than Survival: Prospects
for Higher Education in a
Period of Uncertainty
*The Carnegie Foundation for
the Advancement of Teaching*

Managing Multicampus Systems:
Effective Administration in an
Unsteady State
Eugene C. Lee, Frank M. Bowen

Making Affirmative Action Work
in Higher Education: An Analysis
of Institutional and Federal
Policies with Recommendations
*The Carnegie Council on Policy
Studies in Higher Education*

Challenges Past, Challenges
Present: An Analysis of
American Higher Education
Since 1930
David D. Henry

Presidents Confront Reality:
From Edifice Complex to
University Without Walls
*Lyman A. Glenny, John R. Shea,
Janet H. Ruyle, Kathryn H. Freschi*

Contents

Foreword

The first major assignment undertaken by the Carnegie Council on Policy Studies in Higher Education was assistance in the preparation of a commentary on the ways in which colleges and universities in the United States have been adjusting to stabilized or reduced enrollments and less adequate levels of funding in the 1970s. This resulted in a report entitled *More than Survival: Prospects for Higher Education in a Period of Uncertainty*. As a part of the investigations for that study three special projects were commissioned. One, by Eugene C. Lee and Frank Bowen, involved impacts of the new conditions on multicampus universities. A second, by David Henry, president emeritus of the University of Illinois, concerned the ways in which colleges and universities have adjusted to other stresses and crises over the past 45 years. The third project, conducted under the direction of Lyman Glenny, involved a national survey of the nation's college and university presidents to obtain, firsthand, impressions of the current situation on the campuses.

It is this third project that yielded the enormously rich data base from which the information in *Presidents Confront Reality* comes. In a general way the testimony from the campuses tells a great deal about the ways institutions of higher education adjust to new conditions. But parts of the information are also valuable to students of special fields within higher education—for example, institutional governance, curriculum, administrative technologies, admissions, financing, and academic personnel.

For this reason we are glad that we are able to reproduce the results of the survey in relatively unabridged form for permanent reference.

The Council wishes to thank the presidents and other administrative officers who responded to this survey and, in doing so, ultimately made this report possible. They have not only helped us, but I am sure they have also helped their colleagues by providing reference points by which their own conditions can be assessed. Our particular appreciation is also expressed to Lyman Glenny, John Shea, Janet Ruyle, and Kathryn Freschi for conducting the study and compiling the results for this volume. They have made an important contribution to the Council's deliberations and to an improved understanding of higher education.

CLARK KERR
Chairman
Carnegie Council on Policy
Studies in Higher Education

1

Introduction

During the "soaring sixties" growth in higher education was spectacular, whether measured by number of students enrolled, dollars spent, buildings constructed, or degrees granted. In contrast, the current decade has been characterized by rapidly*falling growth rates in all these dimensions. State and federal budget priorities are shifting. Many observers see the beginnings of an extended period of very little or no growth in total enrollment, with an absolute decline occurring in the 1980s. Today, economic recession and inflation exacerbate the problems of adjusting to the new realities of declining rates of enrollment and of financial support.

Problems

Unless a sharp turnaround occurs in the rate of college attendance, higher education—as presently structured and defined—will require continuing and substantial adjustments during much of the remainder of this century. Because of a projected decline in the number of 18- to 24-year-olds in the population, the "new depression in higher education" is likely to be a long one (Cheit, 1971 and 1973).

Of course even in periods of expanding total enrollment some colleges and universities lose students and resources. This fact, in part, prompted the present report. In the summer of 1974 an instrument entitled "Survey of Presidents' Response to Changes in Enrollments and Financing" was mailed to the presidents of approximately 2,500 institutions of higher education. (The questionnaire is reproduced in Appendix A.) The results of the survey allow us to compare the problems and responses of institutions "in trouble" with those of institutions still experiencing growth.

Procedures

We designed the questionnaire so as to address a number of interrelated questions:

1. What kinds of institutions are most affected by stable or declining enrollments and funding?
2. How are institutions affected? Does a decline in enrollment and funding influence an institution's ability to reform its curriculum? Does it affect the number and type of faculty and staff employed? Does it lead to changes in the quality of students, programs, and faculty?
3. Faced by competitive pressures, do colleges and universities respond in classical ways by introducing new products, adopting new methods of production, exploiting new markets, tapping new resources, or reorganizing their "industry" through consolidation or merger?[1]
4. How is the ability of institutions to respond affected by personnel policies and the locus of general decision-making authority?
5. What general strategies and tactics do institutional leaders expect to use in adapting to shifting levels of enrollments and funding? Specifically, what kinds of planning and management tools do presidents intend to use?

Presidents were asked for their perceptions of change on their campuses between 1968 and 1974, and for their expectations of change over the period from 1974 to 1980. The sample universe consisted of nearly all colleges and universities listed

[1]L. L. Leslie and H. F. Miller, Jr., have recently examined the predicament of higher education in these terms. See their *Higher Education and the Steady State* (1974).

in the most recent directory of institutions of higher education published by the U.S. Office of Education (1974).[2]

Response Rate

Representatives of 1,227 institutions returned usable questionnaires by mid-September 1974, for a response rate of 49 percent.[3] Responding institutions, however, enroll approximately two-thirds of all students in higher education. Except for a lower-than-average response rate on the part of small institutions, respondents appear to be quite representative of institutions included in the sample universe. This is certainly true with respect to the Carnegie typology (defined below) and institutional control, two variables used extensively throughout the report for statistical control purposes (Appendix C, Table 22).[4] Small liberal arts colleges (Liberal arts II), two-year colleges and institutes, and professional schools are slightly underrepresented among our responding institutions. Small, religiously affiliated private institutions,[5] predominantly black colleges, and institutions in the middle Atlantic region and the southern states are also underrepresented (Table 23).

The Carnegie classification categorizes four-year institutions in terms of: (1) level of federally supported research, (2) number of doctoral degrees awarded, (3) level of enrollment, (4) number of kinds of academic and vocational program offerings, and (5) selectivity in admissions. Two-year colleges and selected technical institutes, as well as various professional schools and other specialized institutions, such as maritime academies and graduate centers, are identified separately (Carnegie Commission, 1973).

Throughout the report we have often combined research universities with other doctoral-granting institutions. Compre-

---

[2]For additional details concerning the pretest results and survey procedures, see Appendix B.

[3]Additional questionnaires came in after the cut-off date, but we were unable to include them in our tabulations.

[4]Tables 22 through 100 are in Appendix C.

[5]The HEGIS data permit a further distinction to be made between religious and independent institutions within the private sector.

hensive colleges and universities, regardless of enrollment size, are typically considered a group. Unlike the doctoral-granting institutions, the "comprehensives" generally lack doctoral programs or have extremely limited offerings at this level. On the other hand, they offer at least one professional or occupational program such as nursing or teacher training. While the distinction between comprehensive institutions and liberal arts colleges is not clear cut, institutions in the latter category have strong liberal arts traditions. Some have occupational programs as well, but they are modest in size.

Preview of the Report

The remainder of the report is organized as follows. In Chapter 2 we concentrate on presidential perceptions (and anticipation of change) in: student enrollments, operating expenditures per full-time-equivalent (FTE) student, capital outlays, and deferral of physical plant maintenance. In Chapter 3 we examine shifts taking place in undergraduate enrollments by field of study, and we report on efforts to eliminate (or consolidate) courses and programs, a painful but necessary process for those who wish to reshape the curriculum during a period of level funding.

In Chapter 4 we consider matters of faculty composition (tenured versus nontenured), workload, staff development, collective bargaining, and early retirement against the backdrop of new program priorities, level of funding, and changing enrollment patterns. Changes in program content, deployment of faculty, and modes of instruction are illustrative of the "new products" and "new methods" that Leslie and Miller (1974) discuss in describing how educational institutions, like business firms, may respond to competitive pressure. Chapter 5 examines their argument in some detail by considering new markets, new resources, and reorganization of the industry, in addition to new products and new methods. Recruitment priorities, changes in admissions standards, and student services are discussed, along with responses to an open-ended item in the questionnaire that pointedly asked: "Looking ahead to the next five years, is the character of your institution likely to undergo any radical change, such as merger, consolidation, or closure?"

Chapter 6 considers various planning and management techniques that are often hailed as tools for increasing institutional responsiveness and for acquiring needed resources. Do these new tools help institutions adapt to the new realities? In Chapter 7 we examine two related matters: the shifting locus of general decision-making authority and its consequences for financial support, flexibility in campus use of funds, curricular reform, and redeployment of faculty; and administrators' perceptions of the helpfulness of various master plans.

The seriousness of the new depression in higher education depends crucially on its effects. In Chapter 8 we report on the perceptions of institutional leaders regarding changes being wrought in the quality of students, programs, and faculty. Some see positive consequences. Many others perceive negative effects. Chapter 9 is devoted to a consideration of policy dilemmas, opportunities, and constraints arising from current and projected conditions.

A Note on Technical Matters

As pointed out in text and tables, we often report findings separately by type of institution (Carnegie types) and control (public versus private). In many instances we collapse categories because of sample cases inadequate for separate analysis. On occasion, we consider all four-year or senior institutions (research and other doctoral-granting, comprehensive, liberal arts) together, in contrast to two-year colleges and technical schools. We sometimes restrict the analysis to either private or public institutions where there are few from the other sector. Nearly all liberal arts colleges are private; most two-year institutions are public.

Occasionally we report percentages for all institutions without differentiation. Especially at this global level of aggregation it is well to recall three things. First, each institution is one unit. Consequently, each carries equal weight in calculating percentages despite great differences in numbers of students, expenditure levels, and the like. The second point to remember is that the public and private sectors are composed of a different mix of institutions. Over half (55 percent) the public institutions that responded to our survey are two-year colleges or technical institutes. Only 1 in 12 private institutions (13 percent) fall into the two-year category. Conversely, over half (52 percent) of the private institutions are liberal arts colleges, while less than 1 in 30 (3 percent) of the public institutions are in this category. Less dramatic differences exist in the case of research and other doctoral-granting institutions (11 percent of all public institutions, 6 percent of all private), comprehensives (28 percent and 13 percent), and independent professional schools (3 percent and 15 percent). Finally, for some items in the questionnaire, relatively few presidents responded. This happened, for example, in such curricular areas as agriculture. Tables do present the base (or N) for each percentage, and we have tried to alert the reader in the text to such cases.

Percentages in tables are reported to the nearest whole number. In most instances, reporting figures to the nearest tenth of a percent would be misleading, because the number of observations is so small. If the base has fewer than 15 cases, we have noted this fact in a footnote and have not reported the percentage. "No observations" and percentages of less than 0.5 percent are also indicated in a footnote.

For ease of expression, we use the terms "president," "official," "administrator," and "respondent" interchangeably throughout the report. We have adopted this convention even though someone other than the president actually filled out the questionnaire in about half the institutions (see Appendix B for details).

2

Trends in Enrollment
and Funding

Sharply lower rates of growth in enrollments and funding—
and, in some instances, actual declines—are at the heart of present concern with so-called steady state conditions. Even institutions still experiencing some growth in total enrollment find it
difficult to adjust to changing student preferences for fields of
study. In part, the difficulty stems from the stable number of
faculty and the resulting problem of how to infuse the profes-
soriate with the "new blood" needed to achieve program flexibility that many institutional leaders seek.

This chapter and the following two delineate the nature
of the difficulties that stem from stable (or declining) enrollments and funding. We begin, in this chapter, by describing
the respondents' perceptions and expectations regarding change
in (1) headcount and full-time-equivalent (FTE) enrollments,
(2) real operating expenditures per FTE student, (3) the availability of funds for capital outlay, and (4) deferral of physical
plant maintenance. We compare responses for the past six years
(1968–1974) with expectations for the next six (1974–1980).
Particular attention is paid to differences by type of institution
(e.g., Carnegie typology) and by control (public versus private).
Shifting curricular patterns, and changes in faculty, staff and
personnel policies are discussed subsequently in Chapters 3
and 4.

Enrollment

Enrollment Changes, 1968 to 1974 and 1974 to 1980

Presidents in a majority (61 percent) of the 1,227 institutions that responded to our survey report an increase in total FTE enrollment of more than 10 percent from 1968 to 1974; 17 percent report a decrease of equal magnitude. The number expecting a sizable change in FTE enrollment by 1980 is much less: 43 percent expect an increase and 6 percent a decrease. The "little change" category swells in size to 51 percent, in part because of understandable uncertainty about the future (see Appendix A, Question 1).

Slightly more institutions experienced an increase in their headcount than in their FTE statistics: part-time attendance has been increasing faster than full-time attendance for the past several years. This pattern is expected to continue. For several types of institutions, the difference in proportions of respondents expecting an increase of more than 10 percent from 1974 to 1980 in headcount but not in FTE enrollments is five or six percentage points (Table 1).

As might be expected, institutions that experienced growth in the past six years are more likely than their nongrowing

Table 1. Types of institutions in which the percentage of respondents expecting an increase in headcount enrollment is at least five percentage points larger than the percentage expecting an increase in FTE enrollment, 1974–1980

Control and Carnegie type	Percentage expecting increase of more than 10 percent in		
	(N)	FTE	Headcount
Public research universities	(35)	37	43
Public other doctoral	(32)	35	41
Private other doctoral	(18)	17	22
Public two-year	(329)	59	64
Public professional	(19)	63	68

Table 2. Anticipated change in FTE enrollment from 1974 to 1980, by
change in enrollment 1968–1974 (in percentages of responding
institutions)

		Anticipated future FTE enrollment, 1974–1980		
		Increase		*Decrease*
FTE enrollment		*more than*	*Little*	*more than*
1968–1974	*(N)*	*10 percent*	*change*	*10 percent*
Increased more than 10 percent	(692)	53	43	4
Little change	(249)	25	68	7
Decreased more than 10 percent	(185)	31	58	11

counterparts to expect an increase between 1974 and 1980 (Table
2). Although not shown here, the institutions that expect the
biggest rebound from steady or declining enrollments to increasing enrollments are religious two-year colleges and those in the
private liberal arts category. A follow-up telephone survey last
January of a small sample (11) of the respondents from these
types of institutions reveals that more aggressive student-recruit-
ing and, to a lesser extent, changes in program account for this
optimism.

As might be expected, actual and anticipated changes in
FTE enrollments are not unrelated to a variety of institutional
characteristics. The most striking difference is between public
and private institutions (Table 3). Officials in only 8 percent of
the former but 26 percent of the latter say that enrollments
decreased by more than 10 percent from 1968 to 1974. Antici-
pations differ somewhat less.

In the public sector, proportionately more community colleges (84 percent) experienced growth over the past six years
than any other type of institution. Professional schools (57 percent) lead in the case of private institutions. Perhaps reflecting
the decline in teacher-training enrollments, one in seven public
comprehensive colleges or universities reports a decrease since
1968. In the private sector, actual decreases of more than 10
percent over the same period were highest among two-year

Table 3. Change in FTE enrollment, actual 1968–1974 and anticipated 1974–1980 by Carnegie type and control (in percentages of responding institutions)

Carnegie type and control	1968–1974				1974–1980			
	(N)	Increased more than 10 percent	Little change	Decreased more than 10 percent	(N)	Increase more than 10 percent	Little change	Decrease more than 10 percent
All institutions	(1,169)	61	22	17	(1,135)	43	51	6
Public								
Research universities	(36)	75	25	a	(35)	37	54	9
Other doctoral	(32)	69	28	3	(31)	35	65	a
Comprehensives	(167)	70	16	14	(163)	36	55	9
Liberal arts	(19)	79	16	5	(18)	78	22	a
Two-year	(327)	84	11	5	(320)	59	38	3
Professional	(19)	74	16	10	(19)	63	37	a
Total public	(600)	78	14	8	(586)	51	44	5
Private								
Research universities	(20)	45	40	15	(20)	5	90	5
Other doctoral	(19)	47	26	26	(18)	17	78	5
Comprehensives	(80)	41	30	29	(79)	15	70	15
Liberal arts	(301)	42	30	28	(292)	35	60	5
Two-year	(70)	39	30	31	(66)	59	35	6
Professional	(79)	57	28	15	(74)	44	53	3
Total private	(569)	44	30	26	(549)	35	59	6

[a] No observations.

institutions (31 percent), comprehensives (29 percent), and liberal arts colleges (28 percent). Within the private sector, differences in enrollment changes by affiliation—independent versus religious—vary from one Carnegie category to another (Table 24).

Regarding other institutional characteristics, the following differences are worth noting. Within the public sector, institutions that are part of multicampus configurations (systems, etc.) are more likely than individual institutions to have experienced growth in enrollment (or to have avoided decreases) from 1968 to 1974 (Table 25). Decreases were more likely among: (1) comprehensive and liberal arts colleges and professional schools that do not offer more than a baccalaureate degree; (2) the relatively small number of liberal arts colleges for women and the larger number that offer teacher preparatory or occupational programs; (3) comprehensive and liberal arts colleges with no professional program as defined in HEGIS; and (4) institutions that pursue an essentially open-admissions policy. Some part of these patterns is doubtless related to the recent emergence of an oversupply of teachers and shifts in student preferences, a topic discussed in the next chapter.

Other differences in enrollment experience are related to size and location. First, as would be expected, small institutions are more likely than large ones to have lost enrollment since 1968 (Table 26). The exceptions are research and other doctoral-granting universities and private two-year institutions. Nearly three-quarters of the liberal arts colleges reporting decreased enrollments have under 1,000 students, while only about one-third of those that had increases are this small. Second, a greater-than-average proportion of institutions experiencing little change or decreases in FTE enrollment between 1968 and 1974 are located in small towns or rural areas (Table 27). Finally, a disproportionate number of colleges and universities that have recently experienced steady or declining enrollment are located in the West North Central, East North Central, and West South Central states (Table 28). Reports of the National Center for Educational Statistics show similar findings. One reason for the regional variation is that the distribution of institutions by type is by no means uniform across the country. Both the East North Central and West North Central regions are overrepresented in our sample by private liberal arts colleges (37 percent and 33 percent of the total in each region, respectively). The West South Central region has a rather high proportion of public comprehensive colleges (20 percent). The Mountain and Pacific regions, on the other hand, are represented by relatively more public two-year institutions than elsewhere.

Enrollment Changes, 1971–1973

With a softening of the job market and an end to the Vietnam War and the military draft, many institutions have just recently

Table 4. Change in headcount enrollment from 1968 to 1974 and from fall 1971 to fall 1973, by type of institution and control (in percentages of responding institutions)

Type of institution and control	1968–1974			1971–1973		
	(N)	Increased more than 10 percent	Decreased more than 10 percent	(N)	Increased more than 5 percent	Decreased more than 5 percent
Universities						
Public	(147)	73	6	(135)	40	15
Independent	(64)	55	14	(59)	44	16
Religious	(28)	46	21	(25)	32	20
Colleges (four-five year)						
Public	(130)	72	12	(122)	51	18
Independent	(198)	53	21	(177)	41	25
Religious	(236)	39	32	(220)	30	32
Two-year institutions						
Public	(333)	86	5	(313)	74	11
Independent	(41)	46	32	(40)	38	32
Religious	(37)	41	35	(35)	40	45
Total	(1,218)	63	17	(1,130)	49	21

Note: "Universities" include institutions offering a predoctorate or doctorate degree beyond the master's as the highest level of training. "Colleges" include institutions that offer a baccalaureate, a first-professional, or a master's degree as the highest level of training. "Two-year institutions" offer no more than an associate degree.

experienced enrollment problems. We asked our respondents to "specify the percentage your enrollment (headcount) changed between fall 1971 and fall 1973." Nearly a third report a decrease. Indeed, proportionately more institutions (21 percent) say they had a decrease of more than 5 percent over the two-year period than those who say (17 percent) they had a decrease of more than 10 percent between 1968 and 1974 (Table 4). There is some slight indication that public universities and colleges only recently began to feel the impact of enrollment declines. Considerably more report decreases of at least 5 percent between 1971 and 1973 than decreases of more than 10 percent between 1968 and 1974. The difference is much smaller among the private institutions.

It is instructive to examine the change in headcount enrollment between fall 1971 and fall 1973 of those institutions that report little change or decrease in FTE enrollment from 1968 to 1974 (Table 29). A few reversed earlier enrollment decreases, but by and large enrollments continued to slip. For example, presidents of a third of the 85 liberal arts colleges with lower enrollments say that their headcount statistics went down over 15 percent between 1971 and 1973.

Enrollment Compared to Earlier Projections

The reduction in enrollment growth has been more dramatic than many college presidents and students of higher education expected a few short years ago. Of all institutions surveyed, about half report that their 1974 enrollments fell short of projections made in the late sixties (Table 30). When we exclude the 1 out of 10 institutions that made no projections (or that are new to the higher education community), the fraction jumps to 54 percent. Of those that made projections, the gap between actual and projected enrollment was particularly large among public universities, religiously affiliated four-year colleges, and private two-year institutions.

Even when enrollments increased by more than 10 percent between 1968 and 1974, in many institutions (especially the public comprehensives) the increase was below earlier projections (Table 31). Most institutions that experienced little change or a decrease had planned for a larger student body. We suggest that actions regarding personnel and programs were often taken in anticipation of greater growth. Some of those decisions probably make it difficult now to adjust to the new realities of financial stringency and reduced enrollments.

Why did projections go awry? We asked presidents: "If actual enrollments fell short of projections, what factors account for the difference?" Several recurring themes emerge from their responses. One is increased competition from other institutions of higher learning. Two-year institutions not infrequently mention universities and state colleges, and four-year institutions often name community colleges. One college president refers to "The opening of five new community colleges and two-year institutions." Another notes the "Overexpansion of [the] higher educational system." A second complex of responses centers on changes in student preferences for programs or majors. One official of a liberal arts college comments on the "general trend in engineering." Another on the "appeal of other vocations in contrast to single purpose of the college." A third reason is cost (or price) considerations, such as the rising gap between public and private tuitions. Inflation, high costs, the "money crunch," and other financial matters were commonly cited. Other reasons included "increased preference for coeducation," "the admissions staff," "national enrollment trends," "unrealistic projections," and "end of the war and the draft." This last item was noted as a salient factor by many more of the community college officials than those in other institutions.

Expenditures Per Student

Our pretest suggested that most respondents were able to report expenditures in real terms—that is, in dollars of constant purchasing power. Therefore, in the survey proper, we asked presidents to: "Indicate shifts in your institution's *real* operating expenditure per FTE student (constant $ per FTE student; adjusted for inflation)." Over half of the presidents (55 percent) report increases of more than 10 percent from 1968 to 1974 (Table 5). Slightly less than half expect an increase of similar magnitude between 1974 and 1980. Historically, real operating

Table 5. Change in real operating expenditures per FTE student, actual 1968–1974 and anticipated 1974–1980, by Carnegie type and control (in percentages of responding institutions)

Carnegie type and control	1968–1974				1974–1980			
	(N)	Increased more than 10 percent	Little change	Decreased more than 10 percent	(N)	Increase more than 10 percent	Little change	Decrease more than 10 percent
All institutions	(1,055)	55	39	6	(1,003)	48	49	3
Public								
Research universities	(32)	31	44	25	(29)	21	65	14
Other doctoral	(31)	39	51	10	(29)	24	76	a
Comprehensives	(153)	48	47	5	(147)	36	61	3
Liberal arts	(16)	38	37	25	(15)	33	54	13
Two-year	(297)	53	41	6	(285)	54	43	3
Professional	(14)	b	b	b	(15)	40	60	a
Private								
Research universities	(18)	33	50	17	(17)	23	77	a
Other doctoral	(17)	59	29	12	(17)	35	59	6
Comprehensives	(71)	63	37	a	(67)	63	37	a
Liberal arts	(265)	58	38	4	(252)	45	51	4
Two-year	(67)	66	31	3	(63)	65	29	6
Professional	(74)	69	27	4	(67)	63	34	3

a No observations.
b Not calculated; base less than 15 cases.

expenditures per FTE student have gone up 2.5 percent per year (Carnegie Commission, 1972, p. 4).

It may come as a surprise that relatively more private than public institutions report increases in per student expenditures of more than 10 percent. Increases are also more likely to have occurred among: (1) public institutions not part of multicampus systems, (2) institutions offering the baccalaureate as the highest degree, (3) institutions below average in enrollment size, and (4) institutions pursuing an essentially open-admissions policy (Table 32). These characteristics are not unlike those associated with steady or declining enrollments. Yet little change or a decrease in FTE enrollment is associated with rising expenditures per student primarily in research and other doctoral-granting universities and in liberal arts colleges (Table 33). The opposite is true among comprehensives, two-year institutions, and professional schools.

While we cannot be sure of the reasons for the correlation between decreased enrollment and increased expenditures per student, two possible explanations come to mind. First, many small liberal arts colleges probably encounter serious diseconomies from small-scale production when decreases occur in their enrollments. Second, some of these institutions may retain faculty in anticipation of a resurgence in enrollment growth. With regard to research and other doctoral institutions, political power may be a factor. Regardless of enrollment changes, a smaller fraction of the doctoral-granting universities report increased expenditures per student than other kinds of institutions. One reason for this may be reduced public support for research and development activities.[1] Another may be the realization of greater economies of large-scale production. Still another may be shifts in state government funding priorities to such other types of institutions as community colleges.

As in the case of actual and anticipated enrollments, institutions reporting an increase of more than 10 percent in operat-

---

[1]The current level of federal support is inversely related to change in dollars per FTE student. That is, the greater the federal support, the less the likelihood of having increased expenditures per student (table not shown).

ing expenditures between 1968 and 1974 are much more likely than other institutions to expect an increase of the same magnitude between 1974 and 1980 (Table 34).

Capital Outlays and Maintenance

Building Program

A third measure of so-called steady state conditions is the extent to which an institution is changing the capacity of its physical plant. We asked presidents about the actual (and likely) availability of funds for building purposes as of 1968, 1974, and 1980. Officials were asked to check either "substantial building program," "moderate building program," or "primarily rehabilitation." In 1968, 53 percent of our respondents were funding substantial building programs (Table 35). By 1974, this proportion had dropped to 18 percent. A majority (51 percent) expect to be doing very little, if any, building in 1980. Only 1 in 10 anticipates a substantial program at that time. Of the 1 in 10, one-quarter funded a substantial new building program in 1968 and 1974; three-fifths anticipate a step-up from moderate building or "primarily rehabilitation."

In 1968, a majority of public institutions of all kinds and a majority of independent universities were engaged in substantial new building (Table 36). At the present time, a majority of public universities and public two-year institutions are funding "moderate building programs and some rehabilitation," while over half of the private two-year and independent four-year colleges are engaged in "primarily rehabilitation." In 1980, a majority of institutions expect no construction of any consequence. There are two exceptions: community colleges and the small number of religious universities.

By and large, the availability of funds for capital outlay in 1974 is related to: (1) having a selective-admissions policy, (2) having access to substantial federal funds, (3) above-average enrollment size, and (4) being located in an urban area (if public) or outside such an area (if private) (see Table 37). As might be expected, the availability of capital outlay funds is positively correlated with an increase in FTE enrollment (Table 38). Our data reveal no systematic relationship, however, between building and changes in *real* operating expenditures per FTE student (table not shown).

Deferral of Physical Plant Maintenance

A related measure of financial difficulties is the extent to which physical-plant maintenance has been deferred. Of all institutions in our survey, only 12 percent report "extensive" deferral since 1968. Another 42 percent mention "some" deferral. Only 4 percent expect extensive deferral of maintenance by 1980. Of the 956 institutions that deferred maintenance, 78 percent expect to have to continue to do so in the future.

The extent to which maintenance is postponed is presumably related to changes in enrollments, but our data reveal major differences only in the public universities and liberal arts colleges (Table 39).

3

Trends in Curriculum

According to several spokesmen, many changes in higher education come about through forces external to the academic environment. (See, for example, Kerr, 1964, p. 105; Veysey, 1973). One important area that is subject to these external forces is the curriculum. New subject matter offerings, course elimination and consolidation, program review, and different curriculum strategies often stem from changing student preferences and social priorities. Laurence Veysey reminds us that American academic history has not been characterized by steady growth in all areas and at all times during the twentieth century. "Instead, the story is one of dynamic processes coexisting with static conditions and with still others where an apparent dynamism conceals equilibrium" (Veysey, 1973, p. 47).

In the first section of this chapter, we examine the perceptions of college officials regarding changes in undergraduate enrollments by field of study. We relate such changes to institutional characteristics and to overall enrollment increases and decreases. Both in the recent past (1968–1974) and in the near future (1974–1980), presidents see a trend toward greater vocationalism. We examine this interest in occupational and professional studies in the second section of the chapter. The shift away from the traditional liberal arts has obvious implications for colleges' missions and curricular strategies. The efforts of colleges and universities to maintain flexibility in their programs is considered in the next-to-last section of the chapter. We look at program-review activities and at efforts to consolidate (or eliminate) courses and programs to free resources for other uses.

Curricular Patterns: Past and Future

Undergraduate Enrollments by Field of Study

For each of several disciplinary or subject matter areas at the undergraduate level, we asked respondents whether their institution experienced an "increase," "decrease," or "little change" in enrollment between 1968 and 1974, and what change, if any,

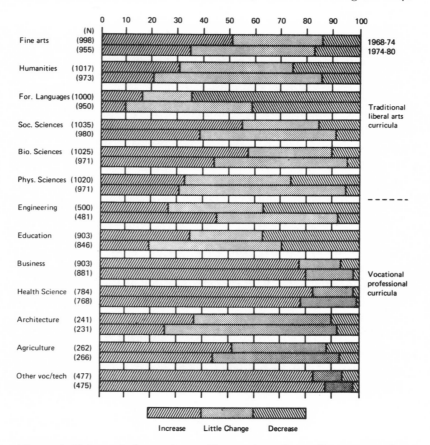

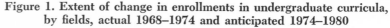

Figure 1. Extent of change in enrollments in undergraduate curricula, by fields, actual 1968–1974 and anticipated 1974–1980

Note: "Other voc/tech" applies to two-year programs only.

they anticipated between 1974 and 1980. The salient findings are presented in Figure 1. Changes over the first time period may be summarized as follows:

- Of the institutions offering work in the following areas, over half report enrollment "increases" in: "other" vocational/ technical (two-year), 81 percent; health sciences, 80 percent; business, 73 percent; biological sciences, 58 percent; social sciences, 56 percent; fine arts, 52 percent; and agriculture, 50 percent.
- Of the institutions with offerings in the following areas, from one-quarter to over one-half report enrollment "decreases" in: foreign languages, 63 percent; engineering, 36 percent; education, 36 percent; humanities, 26 percent; and physical sciences, 25 percent.

The following alteration of trends is evident in projections to 1980:

- An increase in the number of institutions reporting little change in enrollments in all fields of study. With the exception of education, the fields that show the greatest shift to the "little change" category are in the traditional/liberal arts category. There is a rise in only three subject matter areas in the proportion of institutions expecting increases in enrollments:

	1968–1974	1974–1980	Percent point change
Engineering	26%	46%	20
Business	73	74	1
"Other" voc/tech (2-year)	81	83	2

The most recent data available from the *Current Population Reports* of the U.S. Bureau of the Census for October 1966 and October 1972 reveal enrollment trends that, on the whole, are similar to the pattern evident in our survey (Figure 2). Although the data cover two different time periods and lack comparability for other reasons,[1] the following similarities between our data and those of the Census Bureau may be observed:

• Significant increases in health sciences and business or commerce—two vocational/professional areas
• No growth or decreases in education, engineering, and physical sciences

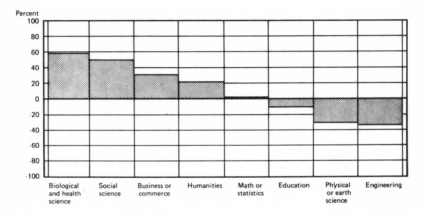

Figure 2. Percent change in major fields of study for college students 14 to 34 years old: October 1966 to 1972 (civilian noninstitutional population)

Source: U.S. Bureau of the Census (1974, p. 1).

Curriculums in Relation to Total Enrollment

The relationship between an institution's total enrollment and subject matter offerings is a complex one. Much depends on the range and concentration of enrollments by field of study. As pointed out in Chapter 2, institutions with teacher-training programs (primarily liberal arts colleges) are somewhat more likely than those without such programs to have experienced a downturn in enrollment. Some liberal arts colleges have doubtless

[1]Our data (1) give institutions equal weight, (2) refer to undergraduates only, and (3) are based on administrators' perceptions categorized broadly into three categories—increase, little change, and decrease. Census data are based on a household interview survey, and refer to individuals in the population.

suffered from the general trend away from liberal arts toward vocational/professional subjects. Some declines, however, have occurred in the vocational realm—notably in teaching and engineering. And, while officials in many colleges and universities expect a rebound in the latter, there is little chance for growth in teacher-training enrollments, a mainstay of many liberal arts and comprehensive colleges.

Interestingly enough, our survey reveals that even if general enrollment declines in an institution, certain subject matter enrollments may increase (Table 40). Despite steady or declining total enrollments, 61 percent of the senior institutions and 40 percent of the two-year schools report increased enrollments in business between 1968 and 1974. Health sciences enrollments increased in 79 percent of these same senior institutions and in 64 percent of the two-year ones. As one would expect, even larger proportions of colleges and universities that have grown in total enrollment report increases in business and health sciences.

Curricular Patterns of Types of Institutions

Table 41 shows the percentage of institutions reporting subject matter enrollment increases by type of institution and by control. In general, more public than private institutions report actual (and anticipated) enrollment increases in the various subject matter areas. Differences from 1974 to 1980 are not expected to be radically different from the earlier period, but a few minor variations are discernible. The percentage of enrollment increases among private, four-year colleges in the biological sciences are expected to fall behind those in public institutions. At the same time, nearly as many private (32 percent) as public (40 percent) expect to gain enrollments in the physical sciences (table not shown). And fewer private four-year institutions expect a decrease in education enrollments than their public counterparts. Among two-year institutions, the gap between the proportion of public and private institutions reporting increases in enrollment is expected to narrow in nearly every field. The only exceptions are engineering and education. The reason for the smaller gap is that many private two-year

institutions expect to reverse enrollment declines experienced
in the earlier period, a matter discussed in Chapter 2.

Senior and two-year institutions also expect different enrollments in the future. Of the private two-year institutions,
39 percent expect enrollment increases in the fine arts compared
to only 23 percent of the private senior institutions. Comparable
percentages in the area of humanities are 19 and 12 percent.
And, quite naturally, more two- than four-year institutions expect enrollment increases in two-year vocational/technical
programs.

Among four-year colleges and universities, enrollment expectations by field of study seem to reflect the differing missions
of the institutions involved. Despite evidence that we shall
discuss in a moment, some liberal arts colleges expect increasing
enrollments in some occupational/professional offerings: 41
percent of the public liberal arts colleges (N = 17) anticipate
enrollment increases in the humanities, compared to 26 percent of all public senior institutions (N = 247). Twenty percent
of the private liberal arts colleges expect enrollment increases in
the humanities, compared to only 12 percent of all private senior institutions. Since the mission of most liberal arts colleges
is to accommodate enrollments in the liberal arts, this pattern
is understandable, especially when one considers the transfer
mission of many two-year colleges.

A large number of private liberal arts colleges (77 percent),
however, also expect to have more students in 1980 than in 1974
in selected vocational areas, especially in business. We suspect
that this forecast and similar ones reflect an interest of some
officials in responding to the perceived preferences of new clientele. For example, 80 percent of the small number of private
liberal arts colleges that responded to the "other vocational/
technical (two-year)" subitem (N = 40) expect increases in this
area. This proportion compares with 69 percent of 63 senior
private institutions that checked the item.

Health sciences, of course, also constitute a growing area
in higher education. Among the doctoral-granting institutions,
64 percent of the private and 93 percent of the public institutions expect enrollment increases in this area. Among the com-

prehensive colleges and universities, the comparable percentages are 70 and 84. Some difference in expected growth may be attributable to the high cost of providing instruction in medicine and related fields. However, in another high-cost area, the physical sciences, the public-private gap is likely to narrow somewhat. Administrators in an increasing number of the private four-year institutions expect increased enrollments in this area.

The Trend Toward Vocationalism

In order to examine in a more comprehensive fashion the curricular directions discussed above, two summary measures were constructed from the 13 subject matter items in Question 11 of the questionnaire. Six subjects—fine arts, humanities, foreign languages, social sciences, biological sciences, and physical sciences—were grouped together under the rubric of traditional/liberal arts. Seven others—engineering, education, health sciences, business, architecture, agriculture, and "other" vocational/technical (two-year)—were grouped together and called vocational/professional studies.

For a summary measure of traditional/liberal arts enrollments from 1968 to 1974, the number of completed responses to the first six subitems in Question 11 was taken as the base. For each institution, the number of "increases" was then calculated as a percentage of the base. The same was done for "little change" and "decrease." Three numbers—each representing a percentage that "increases," "little changes," and "decreases" are of the base—were then added to the data files for each of the institutions. The same procedure was followed in developing summary measures for each institution in the area of vocational/professional studies.

The summary measures confirm the pattern evident in individual areas of study. Only 27 percent of our respondents report increases in more than half of the traditional/liberal arts disciplines in which they offer course work, whereas 52 percent experienced such increases in the vocational/professional area (Table 6).

An examination of the vocational/professional summary

Table 6. Undergraduate enrollment changes in traditional/liberal arts
and vocational/professional studies, 1968–1974 (in percentages
of responding institutions)

Enrollment changes in curricular areas	Six areas in traditional/ liberal arts	Seven areas in vocational/ professional studies
	(N = 1,067) [a]	(N = 1,097) [b]
Increased in more than half the areas	27	52
Little change in more than half the areas	20	15
Decreased in more than half the areas	9	6
No shift in a majority of areas	44	27

[a] Includes 21 institutions with only one area in traditional/liberal arts.
[b] Includes 119 institutions with only one area in vocational/professional studies.

measure by Carnegie typology reveals a number of important differences by type of institution (see Table 42). More public than private institutions report increased vocational enrollments. Seventy-four percent of the public research universities and 81 percent of other doctoral-granting institutions report increased enrollments in over half of their vocational programs, compared with 16 and 40 percent in the two comparable private categories. In the private sector, the greatest proportion of institutions reporting a rise in vocational enrollments is in the professional school, where three-fifths report increases in at least half their vocational areas. Next to the professional schools, where one might logically expect this emphasis, the greatest proportion reporting vocational enrollment increases occurs among the private liberal arts colleges (44 percent).

The growth of enrollments in vocational areas in the liberal arts colleges can be explained as follows. Traditionally, liberal arts institutions have offered few vocational programs other than those associated with teacher-training. For this reason, nearly any increase in vocational enrollments could result in a substantial percentage change. The increased vocational enrollments thus reflect the general upward trend in enrollments in business and health sciences, which have become part of the curriculum in at least half of the private liberal arts institutions that responded to our survey.

There is a question, of course, as to how easily liberal arts colleges can move toward a more comprehensive instructional function, and also whether they should. Liberal arts colleges are more likely than other institutions to face this dilemma: to retain their present concentration in the liberal arts, risk enrollment decline, but maintain a diversity valued in higher education; or to develop and prosper through some creative combination of the new and the old, but possibly sacrifice their unique qualities. It is evident from the data that some liberal arts colleges have already followed one or the other of the two paths.

Overall increases in vocational/professional enrollments are greatest in those institutions that offer work in a medium number of vocational areas. For analytical purposes, we divided institutions into three groups according to the number of vocational areas offered. We call institutions with one, two, or three vocational areas "low vocational," those with four or five, "medium vocational," and those with six or seven, "high vocational." The percentage of institutions in each of these three categories reporting enrollment increases in at least half their vocational/professional areas is shown in Table 7. High vocational institutions are no more likely to report an increase of enrollment in most of their programs than are the low voca-

Table 7. Percentages of institutions reporting increased enrollment in half or more of their vocational programs, by number of areas offered, 1968–1974

Type of institution by number of vocational or professional areas offered	(N)	Percentage of institutions reporting increased enrollments in half or more areas
Low vocational (one to three areas)	(470)	50
Medium vocational (four or five areas)	(284)	75
High vocational (six or seven areas)	(183)	51

tional institutions. Although not shown in the table, a much higher proportion of low vocational institutions report no decreases in any of the few areas offered (66 percent) compared with the medium or high vocational institutions (52 percent and 36 percent respectively). In contrast, the high vocational institutions have the highest percentage reporting more areas with increases than with decreases in enrollment (42 percent). The percentages for medium and low vocational institutions are 31 percent and 10 percent, respectively.

Vocationalism is not an entirely new element in the American undergraduate curriculum. Even in the earliest days of the American colonial college, higher education had a dual mission. The early college emphasized the aristocratic training of the gentleman via a liberal education and the training of clergy (Wilms, 1973). Jencks and Riesman (1968) also remind us that Americans have always been interested in jobs and thus have been inclined toward vocationalism. The relative emphasis on occupational/professional versus liberal studies has always reflected popular moods and the current needs of society.

The reemergence and importance of vocationalism in the undergraduate curricula can perhaps best be attributed to:

- The theme of social relevance born in the late 1960s, which puts a premium on action and improvement of society and oneself, rather than on contemplation.
- The women's movement, which in large part has been directed toward equal job rights for women.
- The entrance of the "new student"[2] into higher education. Such persons are supposedly career-oriented and interested in practical matters and job-related courses.
- A federal government that purposefully funds "career education."
- The changing job market for college-trained manpower. Some graduates without specific skills find it difficult to compete for available jobs.

[2]For a discussion of the characteristics of the "new student," see Cross (1971).

Curriculum and Institutional Flexibility

Since professors are typically specialists, shifts in student preferences, especially under conditions of overall stability in enrollments, have significant implications for program management and for personnel policies and practices. We shall discuss aspects of the former here, but postpone a consideration of personnel matters until Chapter 4. (Shifts in the locus of decision-making authority, another related matter, is dealt with in Chapter 7.)

Course and Program Consolidation

We asked presidents about the extent of elimination or consolidation of courses and programs for purposes of reallocating resources. The difficulty in expanding one area at the expense of another is highlighted in Robert Heilbroner's recent book, *The Human Prospect.* He draws a parallel between the reallocation of resources and loss of freedom in decision-making. Table 8 presents the percentages of institutions reporting "extensive" and "some" course and program elimination or consolidation in both the 1968 to 1974 and 1974 to 1980 time

Table 8. Percentages of institutions reporting "extensive" or "some" elimination or consolidation of courses and programs for purposes of reallocating resources, actual 1968–1974 and anticipated 1974–1980

Type and level of elimination or consolidation	1968–1974	1974–1980	Percentage point change
Courses			
Undergraduate	50	75	25
Graduate	32	65	33
Professional	30	52	22
Program			
Undergraduate	41	63	22
Graduate	30	57	27
Professional	24	43	19

Note: Numbers upon which percentages are based range from 296 to 1,110. See Appendix A, Questions 12 and 13 for details.

periods. College officials expect to do more in the future than in the past.

As one might suppose, course elimination is associated with steady or declining total enrollments (Table 43). Notable exceptions, however, are the private comprehensive institutions and the private two-year colleges, where course elimination is reported by more institutions with increasing than decreasing FTE enrollments. In the future time frame, the correlation continues between anticipated "little change" or a "decrease" in FTE enrollments and course elimination or consolidation, but is less striking. The possible relationship between increasing operating expenditures per FTE student and course (or program) elimination or consolidation is clouded by the underlying positive correlation between decreases in enrollment and increases in dollars per student.

Program elimination appears to occur under different institutional conditions than course elimination (table not shown). Program reduction is least prevalent in liberal arts colleges with little change in enrollments and "little change" or "decreasing" dollars per FTE student, and in public two-year institutions with increasing enrollments and "little change" or "decreasing" dollars per FTE student.

Program Evaluation

Program evaluation is the sole professional/administrative area in which more institutions anticipate increases in personnel in the future than experienced them over the past six years. (See Table 10 in Chapter 4.) Nearly a third of our respondents expect an increase over 5 percent in the number of staff employed in this administrative area between 1974 and 1980. Less than a quarter experienced a similar increase from 1968 to 1974. And, as pointed out in Chapter 6, many more institutions are expected to change their use of program-evaluation techniques: 68 percent anticipate extensive change from 1974 to 1980, compared to 27 percent who experienced such change from 1968 to 1974.

Traditionally, program evaluation has been little more than the ongoing assessment of academic offerings in an effort to maintain institutional vitality. Presently, however, program evaluation may be regularly used in assigning funding priorities and in canceling out some courses or programs. Presumably, greater course elimination in the future will often be accomplished through an orderly process of program evaluation.

Different institutional types report varying emphases on the program-evaluation function (see Table 44). Clearly, a greater proportion of public than private institutions expect to expand the number of personnel in this area: 45 percent compared to 17 percent in senior institutions. Only 6 percent of the private research universities expect an increase. Because of their small size, some private institutions may combine the program-evaluation function with some other administrative area and thus not be registered in our survey. There is little, if any, correspondence of steady or decreasing enrollments with plans to increase program-evaluation staff in the future (table not shown).

4

Trends in Faculty, Staff, and Personnel Policies

Faculty and staff are of central importance to the educational enterprise. They nurture new programs. They provide executive leadership and staff support. They offer instruction and opportunities for learning. Many issues now surround personnel policies as a consequence of steady state conditions. How can "new blood" be added to institutions in the face of steady or declining enrollments? How can the needs of new students and programs be met if new faculty are needed but there is little turnover of personnel? Given the problems of selective reallocation of resources, what is likely to happen to tenure and promotion policies, early retirement, and faculty development? What personnel policies make sense for the years immediately ahead?

In the first section of this chapter we examine presidential perceptions of actual and anticipated changes in the number of faculty, administrators, and other professional staff. Since nonfaculty professional staff (for example, admissions personnel) are discussed elsewhere in the report, the remainder of this chapter focuses on faculty and personnel-related policies. Following the overview, a second section is devoted to faculty changes in relation to overall funding and enrollment levels. The third section concentrates on personnel policies.

Faculty and Staff: an Overview

One important indicator of growth or reduction of an institution is the size of its faculty. Increases in numbers reflect both adjustment to immediate staffing needs and confidence that the future will require their continuance. Faculty members, especially tenured ones, represent a long term financial commitment on the part of the institution. Reductions in numbers of faculty members reflect some previous miscalculation in estimating the future or a response to major programmatic change, planned or unplanned.

Two-thirds of the institutions in our survey report an increase of over 5 percent in the number of instructional faculty between 1968 and 1974 (Table 9). Only 14 percent report a comparable decrease. A majority (53 percent) anticipate little change in faculty size from 1974 to 1980.

Table 9. Percentages of institutions reporting an increase over 5 percent in number of faculty and staff, actual 1968–1974 and anticipated 1974–1980, by level of staff

Faculty and staff	*1968–1974*	*1974–1980*	*Percentage point change*
Total instructional faculty	67	37	− 30
Tenured faculty	69	46	− 23
Nontenured faculty	50	30	− 20
Research (only) faculty	22	15	− 7
Part-time faculty	53	42	− 11
Administrators, upper level	32	11	− 21
Administrators, middle level	45	19	− 26
Clerical staff	60	31	− 29
Maintenance staff	49	31	− 18

Note: Numbers upon which percentages are based range from 992 to 1,180, except for the small number of institutions with research (only) faculty. See Appendix A, Question 18 for details.

Within both time frames, over one-fifth of our respondents report decreases of over 5 percent in nontenured faculty. There are two reasons for this large decline: First, even though an institution may be engaged in little or no hiring, some non-tenured faculty can expect to earn tenure. The second reason is that reductions in force generally involve not hiring new faculty or firing those with little seniority. Both methods affect nontenured more than tenured staff.

Almost 65 percent of faculty in the nation are tenured (Bayer, 1973); by 1980, the figure is expected to rise to 78 percent (Mann, 1973). Rising percentages of tenured and older faculty members may threaten an institution's capability to respond to major societal changes. Robert Blackburn (1972) has reported that the ability to undertake reform, to adapt to social demands, and to perform effectively the job of college instructor has not in the recent past correlated with age and academic rank. But the shift in the future will be of a very different type than the minor adjustments within a discipline characteristic of the past. Faculty members will find great difficulty switching from teaching one discipline to teaching another, although such shifts may be desirable in responding to changing student preferences.

While fewer institutions anticipate increases in total faculty than in the past (67 versus 37 percent), the decrease in the proportion expecting increases in part-time faculty is not as great (53 versus 42 percent). This may indicate a conscious plan to place somewhat greater reliance on adjunct personnel. If so, the expectation is consistent with intentions to recruit and serve more adult, evening, and off-campus students (see Chapter 5 for a further discussion of these intentions). Data for actual and anticipated changes in faculty for specific subsets of institutions in the public and private sectors are presented in Table 45.

For the future as well as the past, fewer institutions report increases or decreases in administrators and staff than in faculty (Table 9). Within the various professional areas, only in program evaluation do more institutions anticipate increases from 1974 to 1980 than experienced them from 1968 to 1974: 31 percent compared to 23 percent (Table 10).

Faculty, Enrollments, and Expenditures

Changes in FTE enrollment are closely correlated with changes in number of faculty. Nearly all public institutions with in-

Table 10. Percentages of institutions reporting an increase over 5
percent in number of professional staff, actual 1968–1974 and
anticipated 1974–1980, by administrative area

Administrative area	1968–1974	1974–1980	Percentage Point Change
Admissions, student recruitment	59	32	−27
Public & governmental relations	33	18	−15
Development, fund raising	44	36	− 8
Instructional & staff development	31	29	− 2
Financial management	38	19	−19
Program evaluation	23	31	8
Institutional planning & research	37	33	− 4

Note: Numbers upon which percentages are based range from 978 to 1,195. See
Appendix A, Question 19 for details.

creasing enrollments from 1968 to 1974 record increases in
faculty. To a much lesser degree, this is also true of the private
institutions. In contrast, the majority of institutions with decreasing enrollments also decreased faculty numbers. Recall
that 17 percent of our institutions report having lost FTE enrollments of more than 10 percent. But only 14 percent report
a decrease of over 5 percent in faculty. Obviously, if these numbers are accurate, some institutions with declining enrollments
experienced *decreases* in student-faculty ratios, and consequently
higher unit costs.

Table 46 shows the difference in the proportions of institutions reporting changes in tenured and nontenured faculty,
based on the changes experienced in FTE enrollments, from
1968 to 1974. Institutions with steady or decreasing enrollments
show either little change or an increase in the number of tenured faculty, but the number of nontenured faculty remained
about the same or decreased. Three out of four of the comprehensive institutions, both public and private, with falling FTE
enrollments also lost more than 5 percent of their nontenured
faculty.

The absence of a perfect correlation between changes in enrollment and the number of faculty is due, in part, to modifications in faculty workloads, which we have defined as faculty-contact hours. Between 1968 and 1974, 7 out of 10 respondents report little change in faculty-contact hours. The remaining respondents divided evenly between those who increased and those who decreased their workload (Table 11). Perhaps because their teaching loads were relatively high to begin with, slightly more of the comprehensive and liberal arts colleges decreased than increased faculty loads, while the reverse was true in other categories.

As indicated in Table 47, nearly the same proportion of public research and other doctoral universities and two-year colleges report increases in number of faculty regardless of whether dollars per FTE student increased, changed little, or decreased. A similar pattern is reported for private doctoral-granting universities. However, among both public and private comprehensive institutions fewer report an increase in faculty if the dollars expended per FTE student stabilized or decreased. Liberal arts colleges show no relationship between faculty growth and FTE dollars. More detail on the relationship between changes in the number and composition of faculty and enrollment and expenditures is presented in Table 48.

Personnel Policies

Personnel policies on promotion and tenure, evaluation of teaching competence, retraining, early retirement, and collective bargaining will become crucial in institutions with stable or declining enrollments—both the total number of students and their distribution by field of study.

Tenure does not grant a person immunity from layoff if financial exigencies or lack of work exist. But there are social, psychological and other reasons why administrators may choose not to lay off tenured staff, even if warranted by changes in enrollment. We asked whether tenure was or would be abolished. Not unexpectedly, only 4 percent of those who responded to the question said "yes" for the period 1968 to 1974; 1 percent said

Table 11. Change in faculty teaching load (contact hours), actual 1968–1974 and anticipated 1974–1980, by Carnegie type and control (in percentages of responding institutions)

Carnegie type and control	1968–1974				1974–1980			
	(N)	Increased	Decreased	Net increase or decrease	(N)	Increase	Decrease	Net increase or decrease
Carnegie type								
Research and doctoral	(101)	20	18	2	(97)	40	3	37
Comprehensive	(234)	17	23	−5	(232)	26	5	21
Liberal arts	(291)	12	17	−5	(287)	29	3	26
Two-year	(363)	14	12	2	(358)	20	6	14
Professional	(94)	20	15	5	(94)	20	5	15
Control								
Public	(554)	17	15	2	(546)	24	5	19
Private	(529)	14	18	−4	(522)	27	4	23
Total	(1,083)	15	16	−1	(1,068)	25	5	20

"don't know." Two-thirds of the 42 institutions responding in the affirmative are two-year institutions. The remainder fall to the liberal arts and professional categories. Over the next six years, 8 percent of our respondents expect tenure to be abolished and 13 percent say "don't know."

Two questionnaire items related to tenure are "rigor of faculty tenure standards" and "rigor of standards for faculty promotions or merit increases." Nearly half our respondents say there was an increase in the rigor of such standards between 1968 and 1974; approximately two-thirds anticipate further increases by 1980 (Table 12). No more than 2 percent report a past or anticipated decrease in the rigor of standards for either tenure or promotion. The somewhat larger proportion reporting on increases in standards among private than among public institutions may indicate an earlier adjustment by private insti-

Table 12. Percentages of institutions reporting increased rigor of standards for tenure and promotions, actual 1968–1974 and anticipated 1974–1980, by Carnegie type and control

| Carnegie type and control | Increase in rigor of standards for | | | | | |
| | Promotion or merit increase | | | Tenure | | |
	(N)	1968–1974	1974–1980	(N)	1968–1974	1974–1980
Public						
Research universities	(36,36)	58	75	(36,36)	58	75
Other doctoral	(32,32)	47	78	(32,32)	34	75
Comprehensive	(170,170)	58	81	(170,170)	56	80
Liberal arts	(20,19)	30	74	(20,19)	35	84
Two-year	(321,316)	34	55	(286,278)	23	44
Professional	(17,17)	35	65	(17,16)	30	56
Private						
Research universities	(21,20)	76	90	(21,20)	81	85
Other doctoral	(19,19)	74	84	(18,18)	72	89
Comprehensive	(80,80)	69	69	(80,79)	66	68
Liberal arts	(305,302)	54	70	(289,283)	51	67
Two-year	(67,66)	39	56	(43,41)	30	44
Professional	(87,85)	46	61	(70,68)	34	57

tutions to changes in enrollments and funding. In any event, denial of promotions and tenure, by maintaining some turnover of junior faculty, can provide some leeway in adjusting faculty resources to changes in the level and composition of enrollment. We can only speculate about the possible impact of such practices on the willingness of able, new Ph.D.'s to seek academic positions.

Presumably, to enhance responsiveness to student needs and to form a better basis for the kinds of personnel decisions just discussed, two out of three college officials report an increase between 1968 and 1974 in "systematic efforts to evaluate faculty teaching competence"; four out of five anticipate a similar change by 1980. Only in the case of private research universities and public professional schools do fewer than two-thirds of our respondents anticipate greater attention to evaluation of teaching in the future (Table 49). As shown earlier in Table 10, essentially the same proportion of institutions in the next six years (29 percent) as during the last six (31 percent) anticipate an increase of over 5 percent in the number of professional staff assigned to "instructional and staff development" activities.

Conceivably, it may be possible to retrain some faculty not needed in one area of the curriculum to teach in another area. Given long years of specialization within the discipline, however, very few observers of higher education are sanguine about this possibility. Nevertheless, new interdisciplinary or problem-oriented curricula frequently emerge that are relevant to persons with various disciplinary interests: for example, (1) chemists and engineers for environmental planning; (2) professors of Spanish and human services for Spanish-speaking populations; and (3) music and dance instructors for therapy for disabled persons. Other faculty redistribution may involve shifts from classroom teaching to teaching off campus in external degree programs, an area in which many presidents see increased emphasis in the future. (See Chapter 5.)

Just over one in five respondents indicates an increase in "systematic efforts to retrain faculty for new or related fields or functions" between 1968 and 1974. A total of 53 percent expect to do more in this area over the next six years. (Less than 1 percent report either actual or anticipated decreases.) With the exceptions of public comprehensive institutions and public research and other doctoral-granting institutions, there is no indication that more institutions with enrollment difficulties than those without such difficulties expect to retrain faculty systematically (Table 50).

Another way to reduce or to reallocate resources is to encourage faculty to retire early. The expectation of continued inflation, however, no doubt makes early retirement less attractive to many faculty than it otherwise would be. Only 13 percent of our institutions increased "incentives for early retirement" between 1968 and 1974; 1 percent report a decrease. (See Appendix A, Question 22.) Forty-three percent expect increases in such incentives between 1974 and 1980. Again, 1 percent anticipate declines. Private research and other doctoral-granting universities have been more active in modifying incentives over the past six years. But in the future, more public than private institutions anticipate an increase in incentives for early retirement (Table 49).

Field interviews carried out with college officials in conjunction with the State Budgeting Study of the Center for Research and Development in Higher Education disclosed more than one instance in which faculty requests to teach one or more years on a part-time basis beyond regular retirement age were denied. This is one illustration of a change in retirement practices emanating from so-called steady state conditions.

Administrators may be constrained by collective bargaining agreements if they attempt to implement tougher promotion, tenure, and workload policies. We asked institutional leaders "to indicate if collective bargaining agreements [were] [would be] in effect at any time" from 1968 to 1974 and from 1974 to 1980, with four types of personnel: faculty, teaching assistants, clerical staff, and maintenance staff. Overall, 13 percent said "yes" to the faculty subitem and less than .5 percent replied "don't know" for the first period (see Appendix A, Question 20). Comparable percentages for the period to 1980 are 32 percent "probably yes" and 16 percent "don't know."

Table 13. Percentages of institutions with collective bargaining contracts for selected personnel, actual 1968–1974 and anticipated 1974–1980, by Carnegie type and control

Carnegie type and control	(N)	Faculty 1968–1974	1974–1980	(N)	Teaching assistants 1968–1974	1974–1980
Public						
Research universities	(36,35)	6	31	(36,36)	6	25
Other doctoral	(33,32)	9	50	(33,32)	a	3
Comprehensive	(169,167)	19	55	(157,157)	6	25
Liberal arts	(19,19)	11	32	(18,18)	a	11
Two-year	(327,320)	28	61	(273,261)	8	26
Professional	(17,17)	17	24	(15,15)	7	13
Private						
Research universities	(21,20)	a	a	(21,20)	a	a
Other doctoral	(18,18)	11	11	(18,18)	a	a
Comprehensive	(78,78)	5	18	(73,72)	a	3
Liberal arts	(310,302)	1	7	(292,280)	1	2
Two-year	(73,71)	6	10	(68,65)	3	3
Professional	(85,81)	4	6	(81,79)	a	1

	(N)	Maintenance 1968–1974	1974–1980	(N)	Clerical 1968–1974	1974–1980
Public						
Research universities	(36,35)	33	63	(36,35)	17	31
Other doctoral	(33,32)	42	72	(33,32)	15	50
Comprehensive	(167,166)	40	59	(168,166)	26	52
Liberal arts	(19,18)	16	33	(19,18)	5	33
Two-year	(324,313)	23	48	(324,318)	17	46
Professional	(17,15)	29	33	(17,16)	18	19
Private						
Research universities	(21,20)	67	75	(21,20)	5	20
Other doctoral	(19,19)	47	53	(19,19)	21	16
Comprehensive	(78,78)	26	26	(77,76)	1	8
Liberal arts	(309,297)	13	17	(309,301)	2	7
Two-year	(72,69)	8	10	(72,70)	3	4
Professional	(83,79)	18	20	(83,79)	6	5

a No observations.

Across the board, presidents say there is both a greater likelihood of and greater uncertainty about collective bargaining in the future than in the recent past.

Considerably more of the public than the private institutions expect collective bargaining contracts in the future (Table 13). Half or more of the public senior institutions expect contracts with faculty, maintenance, and clerical staff. The small proportion of private liberal arts colleges, private two-year institutions, and professional schools expecting bargaining contracts may be a result of the small size of many of these institutions.

The existence of collective bargaining may, however, encourage as well as inhibit changes in personnel policies. Collective agreements may, for example, enhance programs to retrain faculty and to encourage early retirement. On the other hand, collective negotiations might well make it more difficult to reduce employment in fields where teaching faculty are underutilized because of enrollment declines.

5

New Markets, Products, Methods, Resources, and Reorganization of "The Industry"

Broad movements in the level of economic activity exhibit what Leslie and Miller (1974) call transverse progression—that is, temporary slumps below a growth trend line, but sharp movements back across. They argue that higher education will approximate this pattern if the functions performed by the system are "essential to the total social system." Meeting professional and managerial manpower needs has traditionally been such a function. Sponsored research in the post-World War II period has been another.

Yet, from time to time, both functions and structures of higher education have changed. The creation of land-grant colleges and, more recently, community colleges are cases in point. Variation in the birthrate, war, such major economic events as the Great Depression, and changes in social policies have fueled (or slowed) the forces of growth. Open admissions, the GI Bill, and recent reductions in federal spending for research and development illustrate policy factors that have changed higher education. Today, colleges and universities play a role in solving the nation's energy crisis, in conquering major health problems, such as cancer and heart disease, and in providing lifelong learning opportunities for the nation's citizens.

As Leslie and Miller see it, present discussions regarding tenure quotas, nontraditional forms, stepped-up recruitment, and new sources of money indicate that higher education is trying to respond to the slowing growth of enrollments and funding. We have already considered curricular strategies and personnel policies. In this chapter we examine whether colleges and universities are responding to competitive pressures as Leslie and Miller suggest: that is, whether institutions of higher education are seeking to sustain the growth process by exploiting new markets, introducing new products, adopting new methods of production, tapping new resources, or reorganizing their "industry" through consolidation or merger.

New Markets

One way institutions can respond to competition is to step up recruitment efforts and to seek clientele who ordinarily would not be served. Nearly two-thirds of the respondents in our survey report "extensive" emphasis on active recruitment of traditional students in 1974 compared to their recruitment of such students in 1968 (Table 14). Somewhat fewer report having extensively recruited ethnic minorities, evening students, other adults, and persons in other categories. An even larger proportion of respondents anticipates extensive overall recruiting efforts between 1974 and 1980. The most dramatic shifts in emphasis are foreseen for adult, off-campus, and evening students.

Neither public nor private institutions in the several Carnegie categories are consistently ahead of the others in terms of change in recruiting emphasis (Table 51). This is the case for all but traditional and low-income students. Proportionately more private institutions than public report great emphasis on recruitment of traditional students. The reverse is true for low-income persons. This is not surprising, because private colleges rely heavily on tuition and fees to cover their costs of operation, while public institutions (1) are the focus of political pressure,

Table 14. Percentage of institutions reporting extensive change in emphasis on active recruitment of students by type of student, actual 1968–1974 and anticipated 1974–1980

Type of student	1968–1974	1974–1980	Percentage point change
Traditional students	65	70	5
Ethnic minorities	51	52	1
Evening students	41	67	26
Low-income students	39	45	6
Adults over 22	38	66	28
Transfer students	38	56	18
Off-campus students	35	58	23
Early admissions from high school	14	34	20
Previous dropouts	14	31	17

Note: Numbers upon which percentages are based range from 945 to 1,175. See Appendix A, Question 27 for details.

(2) have a mandate to serve the entire population, and (3) receive heavy government subsidies.

In establishing the relationship between an institution's recruitment efforts and other variables, we restricted the analysis to five types of students: early admissions from high school, traditional students, and transfer students, ethnic minorities, and adults over 22 years of age. Those institutions reporting extensive recruiting of traditional students and early admissions from high school between 1968 and 1974 are more likely than others to have experienced a decrease in enrollment and/or an increase in expenditures per student during the same period (Table 52). The same relationship holds among private institutions in their recruitment of adults and for public institutions in the case of transfer students. Thus, there is some evidence that colleges and universities step up recruiting efforts when their enrollments decline. The positive correlation between recruitment efforts and expenditures per student may mean that institutions hold onto excess faculty in anticipation of enrollment upturns.

How systematically do institutions recruit new clientele? Institutions making "extensive" changes in the use of market surveys and needs analysis in 1974 compared to 1968 are more likely than other institutions to have greatly increased recruitment. For example, one fourth of the presidents of private liberal arts colleges say their recruitment of adults in 1974 was "extensive" compared to 1968; over a third report "very little" active recruitment. Among the former, 71 percent made extensive use of market survey or related techniques. Among the latter, less than half did so (Table 53).

In support of recruitment, a third of our respondents expect to increase over 5 percent the number of professional staff in "admissions, student recruitment" between 1974 and 1980. (See Table 10.) Practically no one expects a decrease. Since three-fifths increased their recruiting staffs between 1968 and 1974, a slowing of growth in this area is expected, despite the upward trend in emphasis on active recruitment of various kinds of students. It may be that college officials will "try harder" with existing staffs. Some may plan for greater faculty involvement in the recruiting process. Or as is already the case for some institutions, perhaps more will contract for specialized marketing (for example, recruiting) services.

Colleges and universities can presumably attract students in a variety of ways, only one of which is formal recruitment via visits to schools, career nights, talks to alumni groups, radio announcements, and the like. Program and curricular changes may be important. Another strategy—especially for students of traditional college age—is to improve student services and to make student life more congenial. We asked presidents to indicate any "change in budgetary priority" given to six student services. With the exception of housing, very few institutions (less than 5 percent) report either actual or anticipated decreases in budgetary priority for these services.[1] Relatively more institutions report an increase in priority for financial aid services

---

[1]This finding is consistent with 1972 forecasts using the Delphi technique, conducted under the auspices of the National Center for Higher Education Management Systems (NCHEMS). See Huckfeldt (1972, p. 10).

than in any other student service. (See Appendix A, Question 30.) Somewhat more institutions foresee an increase in academic advising and vocational counseling in the future than report an increase in the past. This may reflect changes in the job market as well as special counseling needs of students who are new (or returning) to higher education. A very large proportion (69 percent) of public two-year institutions report an increase in budgeting priority for vocational counseling. This may reflect increasing counseling to women returning to the work force and to young people with practical interests in careers. Understandably, since a third of the respondents represent community colleges and most four-year institutions have sufficient dormitory space to accommodate today's students, the budget priority for housing has remained the same and for the future more institutions report little change than for other kinds of student services.

One way colleges and universities can confront enrollment difficulties is to modify admissions requirements. We asked college officials to indicate the "extent of modification of admission standards to increase enrollments." Very few institutions checked "extensive" modification for either past or future time frame—at least for the reason stated (see Appendix A, Question 28). Yet, including "some" change as well, two out of five institutions report changes in undergraduate admissions standards (Table 54).

Except for public doctoral-granting institutions, about the same (or a smaller) fraction expects to increase enrollments by changing undergraduate admissions standards in the future as in the past. About a third more of the public universities anticipate changes by 1980: 41 compared to 30 percent. Private institutions are about equally likely as public to have made changes (or to expect changes) at the baccalaureate level. Compared to the past, more institutions in both categories anticipate modifications in admissions standards at the graduate and professional levels to boost enrollments. Nineteen percent of the public colleges and universities with graduate-level programs report "extensive" or "some" modification in standards between 1968 and 1974, compared to 18 percent of the private institutions. Comparable proportions expecting such changes by 1980 are 30 and 25 percent. Despite the trend, these proportions are lower than those reported for the undergraduate level.

Changes in undergraduate admissions standards are mildly related to declining enrollments (Table 55). Changing admissions standards also coincided with increases in dollars expended per FTE student, at least in the case of public institutions. This pattern may reflect a response of budgetary authorities to some of the special needs of educationally disadvantaged students, to adults, and to students "new" to higher education. Modified admissions standards at the undergraduate level are positively associated with increased emphasis in recruitment of adults, transfers, traditional students, early admissions from high school, and ethnic minorities (Table 56). In part, the pattern may reflect the underlying correlation between enrollment declines and increases in expenditures per student, which we pointed out in Chapter 2.

New Products

Despite the impediments to resource reallocation brought on by declining enrollment and financial difficulties, competitive organizations might be expected to develop new products. For colleges and universities, this may mean new degrees, new instructional programs, adaptation of old programs to serve new clientele (for example, taking a program off campus or rescheduling classes), or even a change in the relative emphases given to the primary functions of teaching, research, and public service.

We asked college officials to indicate "change in the number of instructional programs designed to serve" four kinds of "new students." Over half the institutions report an increase in programs for adult, evening, and off-campus students for both time periods and almost half reported increases in the number of programs for ethnic minorities (Table 57). Very few mention decreases in the number of such programs. Consistent with opinion expressed three years ago in the NCHEMS Delphi study (Huckfeldt, 1972, p. 8), presidents report a relative decline in the rate of increase in the number of programs designed to serve ethnic minority groups. Only a third expect to increase programs for ethnic groups by 1980, but nearly three-fourths anticipate a wider array of offerings for adult, off-campus, and evening students. In both the past and future, presidents of relatively more of the public than private institutions increased, or expect to increase, the number of programs for "new students." Since programs to serve new clientele may be expected to prevent enrollment declines or to increase enrollment gains, it is not surprising that there is no consistent relationship between an increase in such programs between 1968 and 1974 and increases in FTE enrollments (Table 58). Nevertheless, except for liberal arts colleges, other private institutions with increased enrollments are more likely than their counterparts with stable or declining enrollments to have increased programs for the four groups of students.

We also asked officials to report the "change in number of instructional programs" at four *levels:* undergraduate, graduate, professional, and extension, evening, and/or continuing education. We interpret the absence of a one-to-one relationship between changes in the number of programs at these levels and changes in the number of programs for "new students" (table not shown) to mean that, in all likelihood, the latter programs often involve rescheduling or slight modification of existing offerings. One half of the presidents say that they added programs to all levels (except professional) from 1968 to 1974 (see Appendix A, Question 14). Few report that the number of programs decreased. Over the next six years, more respondents expect further increases than decreases. But, except in the area of "extension, evening, and continuing education," fewer institutions in the future will increase programs than have in the past. In several Carnegie categories, slightly more institutions expect the number of undergraduate programs to decrease between 1974 and 1980—notably, public and private research and doctoral-granting universities, and private comprehensives (Table 59). Private liberal arts colleges, many of which have especially serious enrollment problems, do not appear to anticipate an array of new program offerings for undergraduates. Twenty-two percent of the presidents expect program offerings to increase; 16 percent expect them to decrease. That seven out of ten expect to have more programs for "new students" probably means that they hope to attract new clientele to existing offerings. (See Table 57.)

Perhaps reflecting the great difficulty of altering instructional offerings via reallocation of existing resources, the expected change in number of undergraduate programs between 1974 and 1980 bears no systematic relationship to earlier change in FTE enrollment or in dollars expended per FTE student (table not shown). However, the facilitating effect of past growth is evident in our data. Between 1968 and 1974, institutions reporting increases in programs at each level are more likely than others to have experienced increased total enrollments (Table 60). Exceptions include public research and doctoral-granting institutions and private comprehensive institutions.

As already indicated, relatively more officials report increases in the number of programs in extension, evening, or continuing education than at any of the other degree "levels." A reason for this difference may be that such programs are easy to mount, involving, as they often do, existing programs and faculty from regular on-campus operations. In any event, while presidents foresee a slowdown in the growth of instructional programs at other levels, more than eight out of ten forecast an increase in their off-campus and evening offerings—a larger proportion than in the earlier period. As might be expected, this change is positively associated with the earlier-reported change in the number of programs designed to serve adult, evening, and off-campus students, and with "extensive" emphasis on recruitment of these kinds of students in 1974. (Tables 61 and 62.)

We have already discussed in Chapter 3 course and program elimination. Although not shown here, "little change" or "decrease" in the number of undergraduate programs is related to more-than-average program elimination or consolidation. This is the pattern one would expect. At the same time, however, institutions that increased their programs in extension, evening, and continuing education are just as likely (and, among some kinds of institutions, more likely) to have consolidated programs and courses as institutions that did not seek to

Table 15. Percentages of institutions reporting increases in funds for
primary functions and support services, actual 1968–1974 and
anticipated 1974–1980

Function	1968–1974	1974–1980	Percentage point change
Primary functions			
Instruction and			
department research	70	59	−11
Sponsored research	26	24	− 2
Public service	46	46	0
Support services			
Academic support			
(library, TV, etc.)	73	59	−14
Student services	70	49	−21
Other institutional support			
(physical plant, etc.)	64	49	−15

Note: Numbers upon which percentages are based range from 962 to 1,208. See
Appendix A, Question 7 for details.

offer more to adults. One plausible hypothesis is that many
institutions that choose to initiate programs for adults couple
this step with a review of existing programs and courses with
the idea of cutting out "dead wood." Another may be that adult
programs were increased for a downturn in enrollment.

Of course, instructional programs by no means exhaust the
possibilities of "new products." We tried, therefore, to identify
major budgetary reallocation among the triad of traditional
primary functions—instruction, research, and public service—
by asking what the "changes in amount of funds" were for these
three major activities. The percentage of institutions that responded "increase" is shown in Table 15. (Few institutions
either experienced decreases or expect them for any function.)
Far more institutions report increases in funds for instruction
(70 percent) than for research (26 percent) or public service
(46 percent). Percentages from one period to the next by Carnegie typology and control do not reveal any startling changes
in mission or activities (Table 63). Not surprisingly, enrollment
increases are associated with reported increases in dollars for

all three primary functions (table not shown). As revealed in
Table 15, the level and direction of change in support services
coincide with variation in instructional activity.

New Methods

Another way that institutions of higher education may respond
to competitive pressures is by altering "methods of production"
—that is, the technology of the teaching-learning process. According to the business-firm analogy, new techniques in production may enable a college to reduce its costs and, thereby,
give it an edge over its rivals. This assumption is, however, only
one dimension of the "new methods" argument—at least as it
applies to higher education. Presumably, some new products
require new methods. Some kinds of professional education,
for example, are best handled via internships. Some nontraditional students are also attracted to the educational enterprise
by opportunities for independent study, small seminars and the
like, as opposed to large lecture classes (Medsker et al., 1975).

More presidents reported "decreases" in the use of lectures
between 1968 and 1974 than reported "increases." (See Appendix A, Question 16.) The opposite is true of other modes of
instruction and learning, with the most pervasive increases being in the self-study and fieldwork categories: Over two-thirds
of the respondents say that they increased the use of these modes.
Over two-fifths report increases in the use of seminars, the next
most frequent category of change. By and large, institutions
see a continuation of the apparent trend away from lecture
classes toward more intimate, more experimental modes of
learning. Although representatives of public and private institutions vary somewhat in their projections, differences in the
anticipated increased use of various methods of instruction are
slight when it comes to (1) type of institution and (2) expected
change in enrollments and funding (Table 64).

Some changes in techniques of production have implications for the ratio of students to faculty. We asked presidents,
"Do you plan a change in the student-faculty ratio? If yes, in
what areas or levels? What would be the change in the ratio?"
All told, approximately 35 percent of the respondents say some

change is likely. Presidents of liberal arts colleges with falling enrollments are more likely than others to answer that ratios will change. This may reflect relatively low ratios to begin with. It may also mean that financial problems must be confronted by reductions in expenditures.

Most of the respondents who say they plan to change the ratio simply note that they expect the ratio of students to faculty to rise. One president states: "Yes. From 10:1 to 16:1 in all areas." Another says: "Yes. Current plans call for the student-faculty ratio to change from 11.6:1 to 13:1 or 13.5:1."

Several officials indicate how they will try to increase "productivity." Basically, their responses indicate an interest in using more paraprofessionals and support staff and wider implementation of media-based or self-directed learning. To illustrate:

Yes. We anticipate approaching 20:1 ratio through greater use of self-teaching practices. Greater use of faculty in smaller ratios in freshman year. Developing independence of student by senior year.

Yes . . . . methods under consideration are: lecture seminar, teaching aides, lab assistants, programmed learning, television lectures, and individualized instruction.

Yes. Through paraprofessionals and hardware we expect to increase student-teacher ratios and reduce unit costs with no loss in quality.

Yes. Greater productivity in lecture (bigger) classes.

No. However, there will continue to be an examination of delivery modes such as technological systems, television, large lectures, etc., which may alter ratios in some areas, not necessarily universitywide.

Another, smaller group of presidents expresses the hope that they can reduce the ratio of students to faculty. Some comments focus on the need to improve quality. Others cite the greater needs of new clientele. Yet others say that this staffing objectives is related to shifts in program emphasis toward the fine arts or occupational training.

Yes. We are bringing the faculty-student ratio back to what it was in 1969 (18:1) and putting more full-time faculty teaching load in evening school—an expensive process but retains faculty and improves calibre of evening school.

Yes. Lower ratio to provide more personalized services to economically disadvantaged students.

. . . [We] see more demands for service to the handicapped, the retarded, those with special learning problems and the like which usually require a smaller student-faculty ratio.

Yes. For professional degrees. Lower student-faculty ratio by 50 percent.

From 17:1 to 15:1 in occupationally related programs.

Yes. It will lower because of growth in programs in the fine arts and in those for nontraditional students.

Yes. Undergraduate vocational programs will increase use of self-learning techniques but this savings will be completely overshadowed by an increase in clinical instructors for the teaching of expanded functions to dental auxiliaries.

A few institutions foresee a change in the ratio as a consequence of changing definitions regarding student workload, faculty, and credit per contact hour. It is perhaps worth reviewing the few comments concerning these artifacts:

Yes. Graduate from FTE = 15 quarter hours to FTE = 10 quarter hours—change requested of legislature. (Policy of one FTE faculty for each 13 FTE graduate students would remain the same.)

Yes. We will attempt to explain the relevant ratio in tenure-track faculty to students, not all prior (e.g., graduate assistant) faculty as well. We'll try this at graduate and then upper-division levels. The immediate effect could be an apparent increase of student/faculty ratio of 20 percent.

No. If any change will occur it will be toward the equating of lab-contact hours to lecture-contact hours.

Yes. Reduce present graduate funding ratios by recomputing FTE graduates from 45 to 30 credit hours per year (or from 15 to 10 per quarter).

New Resources

Leslie and Miller suggest that some organizations may respond to competitive pressure by locating new resources and using them in the production process. By and large, their "new resources" argument focuses on new sources of funds. Large proportions of college officials see continued growth in income from each of their usual sources (Table 16). Only from the local and federal government do 10 percent more of the respondents report decreasing support in either time frame. Presidents of public two-year colleges foresee relatively more of their financial resources coming from state rather than local government in the years ahead (Table 65). Overall, 18 percent of the respondents report less federal support in 1974 than in 1968; 12 percent anticipate declines over the next six-year period. Nevertheless, nearly half (43 percent) expect more federal money in 1980 than they received in 1974. This may be unrealistic in view of the economic circumstances now facing the nation's government.

Officials in many institutions, including several interviewed in the course of the Center's State Budgeting Project, plan to step-up their fund-raising efforts. The most striking trend is in the proportion of colleges and universities, especially in the private sector, that expect increases in funds from: (1) endow-

Table 16. Percentages of institutions reporting more financial support
from various funding sources, actual 1968–1974 and anticipated
1974–1980

Funding source	1968–1974	1974–1980	Percentage point change
Government			
Local	31	30	−1
State	78	70	−8
Federal	51	43	−8
Other			
Endowment	42	60	18
Foundations and corporations	47	57	10
Private donors (inc. alumni)	60	72	12
Enrolled students (tuition and fees)	73	65	−8
Continuing education and related services	59	69	10

Note: Numbers upon which percentages are based range from 505 to 1,163. See
Appendix A, Question 8 for details.

ments and private donors, and (2) continuing education and related services. The shift in recruiting emphasis to adults and
others interested in continuing education is expected to bring in
additional money. Of course, in terms of capital values, many
endowments have suffered greatly as a consequence of inflation.
On the other hand, higher yields from some investment portfolios could mean that endowment income will rise in relation
to other sources of funds. This seems doubtful, however.

Reorganization

Severe competitive pressures have forced a few institutions out
of business in the past. Declining enrollments and rising costs
will doubtless compel many others to reorganize in a funda-
mental way by 1980. We asked officials: "Looking ahead to the
next five years, is the character of your institution likely to
undergo any radical change such as merger, consolidation, or
closure?" Nearly one in eight say "yes" or "probably." Many

others describe the future as very uncertain. There is a natural reluctance among administrators to report the serious problems that many institutions doubtless face.

By no means are the presidents of all types of institutions equally likely to expect "radical change," as they define these terms. Compared with other four-year institutions, a disproportionate number of those in the public comprehensives and private liberal arts II categories expect significant alteration in their activities or structure. Many in the latter category have very small numbers of students—typically less than 1,000.

Institutions with administrators expecting radical change are more likely than average to be: (1) predominantly black, (2) for women only, (3) located in small town or rural areas (if public) or in suburbs or downtown (if private), (4) single institutions unaffiliated with any state system or segment, (5) institutions that follow a policy of "essentially open admissions," and (6) institutions that have lost enrollments between 1968 and 1974.

One radical change involves either closure or merger of two independent colleges to form a new and supposedly stronger unit. Officers in a number of other institutions note their intention of becoming part of multicampus systems. One president states: "We expect to go to a multicampus configuration." Another remarks: "It should become a major senior institution serving the largest metropolitan area (in the state)." Several community college administrators write that merger with an area vocational-technical school is likely. Other four-year and two-year institutions are expected to join existing subsystems of state systems of higher education. In this way, more than one private college is expected to "go public." One cannot help wondering whether these expectations are realistic in an era when the capacity of existing public campuses is less than fully utilized.

Officials in several institutions express a desire for greater cooperation:

There will be a consortial arrangement with two other public two-year colleges and one private college.

Extended interinstitutional cooperation with
state university next door.

Yes—some form of significant interinstitutional
cooperation. Probably embracing consolidation of a
few programs.

Consortium-type arrangements will hopefully
be expanded beyond those presently effected.

One liberal arts college official, however, sees a danger in co-
operative efforts involving his college and an urban community
college located 40 miles away:

The biggest problem facing [us] . . . is the attempt
by the community college . . . to enter into a contract for services. In my judgment, such a contract for
services would make [us] . . . essentially an extension center of a community college. We would lose
our identity and distinctiveness and probably cooper-
rate ourselves out of existence.

Presidents of several institutions refer to closure possibilities. Many worry that enrollment upturns, an end to inflation,
and—among private institutions—more broadly-based financing
patterns will not emerge soon enough to resolve their survival
problems:

Closure is a possibility.

The presumption is "yes" if situation of enrollment does not improve.

Not at this time. We could face merger or closure within a five-year period if we have any unex-
pected sharp declines in enrollment or major unfore-
seen expenses.

Closure is a distinct possibility for a small, un-
endowed [institution] . . . trying to survive in an
inflationary economy which devalues what liberal
education values.

Possibly closure if we can't find dollars and students which require extreme changes in program.

Possibly, if inflation continues unchecked and government support is withheld from private institutions such as ours.

Merger is unlikely, given our location; consolidation of personnel and programs is already an ongoing process on this single-campus institution. Closure is a real possibility, and one we have to face up to; better to close than to become marginal in programs and in what our degree stands for. It is easier to make that statement dispassionately under these circumstances than to contemplate its meaning in terms of history and human lives. Additional state assistance for students selecting independent colleges could make an enormous difference, as could institutional help such as is given in New York. I believe that both could be given without jeopardy to any constitution (although I am not so sure about lack of jeopardy to the independence of the institution).

6

Management Techniques and Practices

Some responses to steady state conditions are piecemeal and un-planned. Others no doubt reflect analysis of alternatives, a weigh-ing of likely consequences, and attempts to develop consensus within the institution. We examine in this chapter the use of various management and planning techniques. Beyond an over-view of nearly a dozen devices—such as faculty-workload studies and simulation techniques—the focus is on four specific items: management informations systems (MIS), unit-cost studies, WICHE-NCHEMS[1] products, and outside performance audits. We discuss interrelationships among techniques and the rela-tionship of MIS and cost studies to (1) changes in enrollment and expenditure, and (2) course and program consolidation. The last section of the chapter describes regional variation in the use of various tools. In the following chapter, we shall con-sider shifts in the locus of decision-making authority and mas-ter planning.

Background

The whole array of management techniques, information sys-tems, unit-cost and workload studies seems newly invented to

[1]The National Center for Higher Education Management Systems at the Western Interstate Commission on Higher Education, Denver, Colorado.

many young systems-developers and analysts. However, many college deans and vice-presidents were using these ideas 20 and even 30 years ago, albeit with less refined definitions and less systematic analysis. The idea that institutions of higher education ought to employ such tools systematically in day-to-day management and long-range planning gained popularity in the 1960s with the burgeoning size and complexity of programs. By the end of the decade, some statewide coordinating agencies and governing boards were using sophisticated management information systems and unit-cost analyses in planning and budgeting for public institutions. A group at the University of Toronto (CAMPUS) had developed a fairly complete set of information and management packages for higher education institutions. The Western Interstate Commission on Higher Education (WICHE) created an organization with similar objectives, which in the 1970s became known as the National Center for Higher Education Management Systems (NCHEMS). Yet another organization, College and University Systems Exchange (CAUSE), was established to expedite the flow of information about the strengths, weaknesses, and uses of various techniques, models, and practices.

Recently, NCHEMS has placed new emphasis on state models in order to improve the management capacity of coordinating agencies and budget offices. Such action logically follows from the increase in number of coordinating boards in 1960s. As enrollments and funding have leveled off for many institutions, state governments as well as institutions apparently see the need for even greater use of the products of management science.

Change in Use of All Techniques

We included in the questionnaire nearly a dozen items under the rubric of planning/management techniques, and asked the presidents to indicate the extent to which the use of each one had changed between 1968 and 1974 (actual) and 1974 to 1980 (expected). Respondents were asked to check "extensive," "some," or "very little." We should be aware that questionnaires were filled out by not only presidents but also by deans, institutional research officers, and others. This caveat is important, because responses reveal little "extensive" change in use of most techniques. Technical staff say that administrators don't always know the extent of use of management techniques.

Of the 11 specific tools listed in the questionnaire (see Questions 31 and 32, Appendix A), only two were mentioned by a third or more of the respondents as having changed extensively in their use between 1968 and 1974: electronic data processing (47 percent) and analysis of institutional goals (36 percent). (See Table 17.) Relatively few institutions changed their use of simulation techniques, WICHE-NCHEMS products, and outside program-performance audits. The use of all techniques, however, is expected to increase sharply. Thus, it appears that,

Table 17. **Change in use of various planning or management techniques,**
actual 1968–1974 and anticipated 1974–1980 (in percentages of
responding institutions)

Planning/management techniques	1968–1974			1974–1980		
	Exten-sive	Some	Very little	Exten-sive	Some	Very little
Management information system (MIS)	26	47	27	55	38	7
Unit-cost studies	22	52	26	55	39	6
WICHE-NCHEMS products	13	36	51	32	46	22
Program-performance audits	11	41	48	21	54	25
Electronic data processing	47	39	14	58	37	5
Faculty workload studies	24	58	18	49	47	4
Program budgeting/ management by objectives (MBO)	17	46	37	47	43	10
Simulation techniques	5	26	69	18	48	34
Analysis of institutional goals	36	51	13	63	34	3
Program evaluation	27	57	16	68	30	2
Market survey, needs analysis	13	49	38	48	43	9

Note: Numbers upon which percentages are based range from 947 to 1,166. See Appendix A, Questions 31 and 32, for details.

for whatever reason, more and more institutions are using specialized tools for planning, management, and accountability.

Responses to the various items are not terribly dissimilar among institutions even when disaggregated by Carnegie typology and institutional control. Roughly comparable proportions of public and private institutions report extensive change between 1968 and 1974 in use of MIS, performance audits, program evaluation, and analysis of institutional goals (Table 66). On the other hand, generally more public than private institutions say that they made extensive changes in use of the other four techniques shown in the table: unit-cost studies, WICHE-NCHEMS products, program budgeting/management by objectives (MBO), and faculty-workload studies. Administrators in research and other doctoral-granting universities and in comprehensive institutions are somewhat more likely than heads of other institutions to have modified extensively the use of MIS, unit-cost studies, WICHE-NCHEMS products, and faculty workload studies. In the areas of program budgeting/MBO, program evaluation, performance audits, and analysis of goals, two-year institutions and/or liberal arts colleges are equally (if not more) likely to have made changes. A part of this pattern is probably attributable to differences in the size and complexity of institutions.

Management Information Systems (MIS)

We have no clear and commonly accepted definition of MIS. In practice, one man's (or institution's) MIS may look like utter chaos to another. The "back of the envelope" data base and the "armchair of the president" computer may serve well many of the smaller, single-purpose institutions.

Be that as it may, perceptions of "extensive" change in the use of MIS from 1968 to 1974 are correlated with FTE enrollment increases of more than 10 percent, which suggests that growth may spur the development of management information systems (Table 67). Three-quarters of the administrators in senior public institutions reporting extensive change in use of MIS tell us that their FTE enrollments increased by more than

10 percent. The same is true of only half of those that made very little change in MIS usage.

Our data reveal that institutions making extensive changes in the use of MIS over the past six years are *less* likely than others to have had expenditures per FTE student rise by more than 10 percent (Table 68). They are also more likely to say that expenditures per student declined by that much. This inverse correlation is especially striking in the case of senior public universities and colleges. Thirty-eight percent of the presidents of these institutions who report extensive change in MIS experienced increases in dollars expended per student of more than 10 percent. Fifty-seven percent of those who made very little change had expenditure increases of this magnitude.

What conclusion can be drawn from such relationships? Can it be that the more information available about an institution, the less capability it has for generating more dollars per student? Or, are institutions that are losing their level of support turning to MIS as one means of arresting the trend? Or, does the relationship simply reflect the underlying inverse correlation between enrollment and expenditure changes? These questions should caution those who advocate the generous use of MIS as a means of proving to funding sources that an institution is accountable and willing to lay its cards on the table. Perhaps they have done just that, and lost the pot. Further research on this matter is badly needed.

As pointed out in Chapter 3, extensive elimination or consolidation of courses and programs for purposes of reallocating resources has not been common in the past. Consolidation has been somewhat greater among institutions with downturns in enrollments than among those reporting increases. Since degree of change in MIS is inversely correlated with the likelihood of a large enrollment increase, it is somewhat surprising to see that degree of change in the use of MIS is positively related to extent of course and program consolidation at all levels of study (Table 69). The correlation of MIS with course changes is greater than between MIS and program changes. In contrast, among public two-year institutions reporting extensive change in MIS, extensive or some consolidation of courses and programs at least at one level (undergraduate, graduate, or professional) is reported by 48 percent of the presidents, respectively. Among those who say that there was very little change in the use of MIS, the comparable proportions for actual and anticipated consolidation are 43 percent and 37 percent.

Does the existence of a management information system have an impact on the degree of flexibility over campus use of funds from state government? While we cannot be sure of the reason for the statistical relationships, greater flexibility between 1968 and 1974 in use of funds is related to degree of change in use of MIS (Table 70) in some institutions. Public two-year institutions are an exception, which may be explained by the increasing importance of state as opposed to local government funding for these colleges. Among the senior public institutions shown in Table 70, presidents reporting very little change in MIS are more likely than others to say that they have less flexibility in campus use of funds from state government in 1974 than they had in 1968. On the whole, presidents of private institutions responding to the flexibility question report that there has been little change in their control over use of state money. The public-private difference may reflect state financial aid to private institutions through grant devices and student aid programs, which are not subject to the state controls usually associated with direct appropriations to institutions.

Unit-Cost Studies

Defining "unit costs" is less difficult than defining MIS. Nevertheless, the term is so vague that a president can take his total operating budget and divide by the total number of students to get "cost per student." Just as with MIS, the sophisticated technician would abhor the "garbage" bias that such procedure entails. Yet for the small institution, trends in cost per student may provide as much guidance for policy-making as the elaborate (and expensive) systems approaches to costing established by some of the large universities and state coordinating agencies.

Unit costs taken at various instructional and organizational levels undoubtedly provide the institution with a useful tool for managing resource allocations and assessing the workloads of departments and programs. Such unit costs are much less useful for coordinating agencies and state budget offices (Glenny,

1974–75). However, these agencies have found that certain cost data contribute to the review of both old and new programs and to the development of budget formulas and guidelines. Some theorists now advocate cost-benefit analyses—in other words, that costs be attached to ultimate "products" or "outputs" (that is, to number of degrees conferred or to job placement rates or even to social adjustment of the graduate) rather than to such organizational variables as departments or to student credit hours. Not much practical progress has been made in these directions by even the most ardent and sophisticated educators and analysts.

As indicated in Table 17, the pattern of response to the question on changes in the use of unit-cost studies is practically the same as for MIS. Twenty-two percent of the presidents report extensive change in its use between 1968 and 1974; 55 percent expect extensive change by 1980. The two variables—MIS and unit-cost studies—are cross-tabulated in Table 71. The correlation is high, but by no means perfect. For example, 22 percent of the senior public institutions shown in Table 71 that made very little change in use of unit-cost studies between 1968 and 1974 report an extensive shift in the use of MIS. And, of those that made an extensive change in unit-cost studies, 1 percent report very little change in MIS. Among private colleges and two-year institutions, the comparable figure is approximately 10 percent—so low that one suspects they may use an "envelope" data base or an "arm chair" computer. Or, their MIS may be ad hoc or a single special study.

The correlations between changes in use of unit-costs and dollars expended per FTE student reveal contrasting results for the public senior institutions and the private universities and comprehensive colleges. Public senior institutions making extensive changes in use of cost studies are less likely than those making very little change to have increased dollars per FTE student by more than 10 percent (Table 18).[2]

Among private universities and comprehensive colleges,

[2] The Center's continuing study of state general-revenue appropriations for higher education reveals that the dollars per student are not being maintained in large state universities at as high a level as they are in the other kinds of institutions.

Table 18. **Change in real operating expenditures per FTE student, 1968–1974, by change in use of unit-cost studies, by Carnegie type, and control (in percentages of responding institutions)**

| | | Change in expenditures per FTE student | |
Change in use of unit-cost studies	*(N)*	*Increased more than 10 percent*	*Little change, decreased more than 10 percent*
Universities & comprehensive colleges			
Public			
Extensive	(69)	38	62
Some	(106)	47	53
Very little	(40)	48	52
Private			
Extensive	(25)	64	36
Some	(56)	59	41
Very little	(23)	43	57
Public & private liberal arts colleges			
Extensive	(39)	62	38
Some	(138)	56	44
Very little	(85)	58	42
Public two-year institutions			
Extensive	(65)	49	51
Some	(157)	60	40
Very little	(59)	42	58

those making extensive change in the use of unit-cost studies are more likely than others to have had an increase in dollars per student. In the other types of institutions, those reporting extensive change are just as likely to report increases as decreases in expenditures per student. The total pattern of responses is puzzling but may be partially explained. Unit-cost studies are often required of the public institutions by a state budget office or coordinating agency which may use the results to reduce dollar allocations per student while the private university studies unit costs primarily to combat the rise in per student costs caused by falling enrollments. Recognizing that correlations do not establish cause and effect, it could be that the systems analysts who advocate more extensive use of unit-cost data may in fact be asking for reduced expenditures per student in the public senior institutions.

Presumably, if unit-cost studies are helpful to an institution, it is in program evaluation and academic management that their influence is felt. The correlation between change in use of unit-cost studies over the period from 1968 to 1974 and change in program evaluation is considerably weaker than that between the unit-cost studies and MIS. Nevertheless, it is positive and moderately strong (Table 72). Happily, the responses suggest that analyses of costs are only one element in the program-evaluation process.

As in the case of MIS, change in the use of unit-cost studies is positively related to extensive or some course and program consolidation at all levels of study (Table 73). Private institutions, which have had some difficulty with enrollments in recent years, have reduced courses more than public institutions. The relationship of extensive changes in unit-cost studies to reductions in courses and programs is fairly substantial except in the program area for private universities and comprehensive colleges.

WICHE-NCHEMS Products

In assessing the degree to which institutions have changed their use of various management techniques, we asked specifically about WICHE-NCHEMS products. We sought the relationship of their use to the development of MIS, unit-costing, workload studies, and program evaluation.

The WICHE-NCHEMS effort to produce techniques, models, guidelines, and structures for management purposes are the most intensive of any organization in the nation, far exceeding any other in terms of funding, personnel, and scope of involvement of field representatives. While the initial efforts of WICHE-MIS in 1968 were confined to the Western states plus Illinois and New York (the latter two because of advanced work in unit costing and MIS), the program was viewed from its inception as a national effort by both practitioners and scholars.

The title of the organization was soon changed to the National Center for Higher Education Management Systems (NCHEMS) and was partially divorced from control by the directors of WICHE. Its executive and technical committees became national in membership. The expectation—then and now—is that NCHEMS products will have a profound effect on management practices in higher institutions.

As pointed out in Table 66, a considerably larger fraction of public than private institutions have changed their use of WICHE-NCHEMS products since 1968. Considering all institutions, nearly half made "extensive" or "some" change in their use; nearly eight in ten anticipate at least some change by 1980.

Since WICHE-NCHEMS products cover a variety of topics (unit-costing, faculty workload, etc.), it should come as no surprise that the correlation is rather high between responses to the question about NCHEMS use and answers to questions about the use of other management techniques. (The techniques, in other words, are not mutually exclusive. On the contrary, there is a great deal of overlap in many cases.) Table 74 describes the changes in the use of WICHE-NCHEMS products and in MIS, unit-cost studies, and faculty-workload studies. The positive correlation over the period 1968 to 1974 is striking.

Change in program evaluation is another matter. The positive correlation with WICHE-NCHEMS products continues to hold, but is considerably weaker, suggesting that WICHE-NCHEMS products may help in the program-evaluation process but are not the sole tool for program review and analysis (Table 75).

Looking toward 1980, presidents of public institutions anticipate a rather dramatic change in the use of WICHE-NCHEMS products. Presidents of private institutions, on the other hand, expect less change (Table 76). Thus, the gap in usage between public and private institutions is likely to rise. Of the presidents who reported very little change in use of WICHE-NCHEMS products between 1968 and 1974, the following proportions expect at least some change over the next six years:

Public research, other doctoral and comprehensive	81%
Private research, other doctoral and comprehensive	60
Private liberal arts	48
Public two-year	65

There is no evidence of disenchantment with the products. It appears to be only a matter of time before the majority of institutions across the country make use of WICHE-NCHEMS products.

Outside Program-Performance Audits

Program-performance auditing by outside agencies is a relatively new concept in higher education, but has quickly taken on meaning for many presidents and other officers of colleges and universities. When the item was placed in the questionnaire, we thought of it primarily as an audit of particular program offerings to determine how well program objectives had been achieved. Some of our respondents, however, probably interpreted the phrase to mean assessments made by accrediting agencies or check-ups by state agencies of how funds are used.

Presidents report relatively little change in outside program-performance audits over the last six years (see Table 17). The proportion reporting little change in use of this technique is exceeded only by similar responses to the use of simulations and WICHE-NCHEMS products among the 11 items in the survey. Between 1974 and 1980, only one in five presidents expects an extensive shift in outside performance-auditing.

We are somewhat surprised that the percentage of institutions expecting more program-auditing in 1980 is not a great deal higher than it is. In the Center's State Budgeting Study, we found, in our sample of 17 states, that governments in 11 states have recently either set up new agencies or given responsibility for performance-auditing to an existing agency. The trend is probably too new for administrators to have either first-hand knowledge of it or to assess its consequences.

As indicated in Table 77, there is a moderate, positive relationship between extent of change in audits and change in MIS and unit-cost studies between 1968 and 1974. Some of the outside auditing is doubtless a function of complex accountability relationships between institutions and state agencies. Some, however, may reflect accreditation processes and use of outside experts in the analysis of program options.

Regional Variation in Use of Management Techniques

There are sizable differences among types of institutions in the extent to which they have changed their use of the four planning/management techniques just discussed. Regional variation within each category, however, is relatively small. Thus, change in the use of various management tools is a pervasive phenomenon, by no means limited to the Mountain and Western States in the WICHE domain.

Table 78 shows the percentages of institutions reporting extensive, some, and very little change in their use of the four techniques by region of the country. The following patterns are worth noting:

- Measured by the percentage that made at least some change between 1968 and 1974, more institutions in the Great Lakes/Plains region than institutions elsewhere have been active in the areas of MIS, unit-cost studies, and WICHE-NCHEMS products.

- Presidents of institutions in the West/Southwest region are more likely than others to report "little change" in use of the various techniques. This is particularly the case for doctoral-granting universities and for comprehensive institutions, regardless of control.

- The pattern of outside program-performance audit is not highly correlated with patterns in the use of other techniques.

Perhaps the most ironic finding in the regional data is that the proportion of institutions reporting extensive changes was lowest in the West/Southwest region, where the WICHE-NCHEMS efforts were developed.

Why should the Great Lakes/Plains region be ahead of others in adoption of MIS and other management techniques? In 1954, the Ford Foundation funded a three-year cost study of the Big Ten universities and the University of California. The purpose was not to obtain cost data, but to develop methodologies and procedures for effective unit-costing. It was hoped that the practices developed from the study would encourage the participating universities to continue their methods of costing to improve internal management. Nevertheless, the study was not considered a success. Several institutions withdrew when the study began to produce actual unit-cost data. The universities were wary about revealing their costs to each other without a guarantee of confidentiality, especially from state political officials.

These university cost-accounting efforts led directly to the studies undertaken by the state coordinating agencies during the 1960s. Practices, procedures, and definitions of cost-accounting were altered in these studies to suit state and institutional purposes, with the goal of obtaining comparable data among all state-supported institutions within the state. These data became the basis for program reviews and for facets of budget formulas and guidelines. Paralleling the development of unit-costing was the formation of the Association of Institutional Research, composed primarily of researchers in the Midwest. The University of California also continued to conduct unit-cost studies, but the practice was not adopted widely by other institutions in California or the West. The genesis of sophisticated management techniques is evident in the regional data to this day.

7

Shifts in Decision-Making Authority and Master Planning

A common assumption held by faculty and administrators is that centralization stifles innovation and flexibility. Many leaders of public colleges and universities feel that administrative authority is shifting from campuses to state agencies. Planning, especially so-called master planning at the state level, has become increasingly important for all types of institutions. Such plans are designed to establish program and degree priorities, building needs, and resource requirements. The federal government recently put additional pressure on the states to plan for all of postsecondary education through so-called 1202 commissions, which were authorized by the Education Amendments of 1972 and encouraged in 1974 by small federal grants to each state.

We asked administrators to tell us whether shifts had occurred in the locus of general decision-making authority between 1968 and 1974 and what is expected from 1974 to 1980: (1) from departments to campus administration, (2) from the campus to a system board, (3) from a system board to a coordinating agency, (4) from a system board to state budget and finance (the governor), and (5) from a board to the state legislature. We also asked about the "effect on your institution of . . . master plans" at institutional, system, and statewide levels.

In the first section of this chapter, we describe the overall pattern of responses to these two questions. In the second section, shifts of authority between department and campus administrations are discussed in terms of: (1) differences by type of institution and (2) the possible effects of shifts in authority in reallocation of resources via course (and program) elimination or consolidation. The third section contains a discussion of shifts in power to (and from) state-level agencies and branches of government.[1] We examine how presidential perceptions of such shifts relate to: (1) changing authority relationships on campus, (2) programs for "new students," (3) flexibility in campus use of state funds, and (4) use of management information systems. Master plans are explored in the fourth section. We focus on the relationship between master plans and (1) whether an institution is affiliated with a system, (2) changes in FTE enrollments, (3) receipt of state funds, and (4) use of management information systems. The last section examines regional and state variation in shifting authority relationships and in master plans.

Overview

Nearly all administrators from whom we received questionnaires responded to the question concerning shifts in general decision-making authority on campus. Only about half, however, answered our queries regarding shifts to system boards and to state government branches and agencies. Understandably, most presidents of private institutions did not respond to these subitems.

A majority of the respondents report that no shift took place in the locus of general decision-making authority between 1968 and 1974 (see Appendix A, Question 38). Except for shifts

---

[1] Since another monograph in the Carnegie Council series, by Lee and Bowen (1975), focuses on state systems of higher education, we do not discuss shifts in authority from campuses to system boards. Nor do we look at the perceived effect of system plans on institutions. We have shared our survey data with the two authors.

from department to campus administration, the percentage of presidents who report shifts in authority to upper levels far exceeds the fractions mentioning decreases in such shifts. Twenty-two percent say that authority has moved from departments toward campus administrations; 21 percent say the shift from departments to campus decreased, which we interpret to mean a shift in power to departments.

The largest reported shift (45 percent) over the last six years has been from system board toward the executive branch of state government. These perceptions parallel the general increase in gubernatorial power in most state affairs. A smaller proportion of respondents reports a shift from system to the legislature (37 percent), from the campus to a system governing board (35 percent) and from a board to a coordinating agency (33 percent). This latter proportion is surprisingly small in view of an abundant literature that reveals a near obsession among institutional leaders who assert that campuses have given up considerable power to state coordinating agencies. The literature may reflect more anxiety than reality. Or, it may be that the roles of the governor and the legislature are viewed as legitimate, while the newer coordinating agencies may be seen as a wall between institutions and traditional centers of power.

From 1974 to 1980, presidents foresee relatively little change in authority relationships on campus, but continued shifts in power from the campus to higher levels. The greatest change is anticipated in the direction of coordinating agencies: an increase of 48 percent between 1974 and 1980, compared with 33 percent over the earlier period. Very few decreases in shifts are foreseen at any level—the highest being 11 percent from department to campus administration.

With respect to master plans, many more institutions report having an institutional than a system or statewide plan, and a higher fraction feel that the former has helped than did those having plans at higher levels (see Appendix A, Question 37). However, a much larger proportion report system and statewide plans have "helped" rather than "hindered," but about one-third report "no effect." For the future (1974–1980), relatively more presidents anticipate that they will have such plans and that those plans will be helpful. We shall look at master planning in greater detail later in the chapter.

Shifts in Authority on Campus

For the period 1968 to 1974, there are few differences in perceptions of shifts in authority on campus by type of institution and control (Table 79). Perceptions of increases in shifts from department to campus administration exceed perceptions of decreases by six percentage points for doctoral-granting universities and private two-year institutions. The percentage of "decreases" is equal to (or larger than) "increases" among comprehensive institutions, private liberal arts colleges, and public two-year institutions. Except in the two-year category far more administrators expect shifts in authority from departments to campus administrations by 1980 than expect the reverse. The gap exceeds 20 percentage points among public doctoral-granting universities and private comprehensive colleges and universities.

One might reasonably assume that centralization of authority is partly a function of enrollment size. Large organizations are more complex and bureaucratic than small ones. Although not shown here, 33 percent of the presidents of public senior institutions with enrollments under 5,000 report a decrease in the authority of campus administrations vis-à-vis departments; only 14 percent report increases. Of the institutions in the 5,000 to 20,000 range, the percentages of "increases" and "decreases" are about the same. Only among public universities and colleges with over 20,000 students do "increases" in campus authority substantially exceed "decreases": 39 percent compared to 9 percent.

While our data on senior public institutions tend to confirm the supposition that size brings centralization of authority on campus, among other types of institutions the reverse pattern holds (table not shown). Among private liberal arts colleges, for example, presidents of institutions with fewer than 1,000 students are more likely to report authority shifts to campus administrations than report shifts to departments. In institutions with more than 1,000 students, more presidents report decentralization than centralization. Among public two-year institutions with enrollments below 2,500, about equal numbers report centralization and decentralization, but among those with enrollments above 2,500, twice as many presidents indicate decentralization as centralization. The large two-year colleges reflect the tendency for large urban systems to create departments and then to allow more faculty participation in governance and decision-making than has traditionally been the case.

In addition to size and tradition, decision-making authority might shift toward campus administrators to facilitate reallocation of resources among programs. Although the data are not shown here, reported shifts in authority on campus are essentially unrelated to course or program consolidation, with two possible exceptions. Among liberal arts colleges, greater authority in campus administrations is correlated weakly with consolidation of courses and programs. Among two-year institutions, centralization is related slightly to course elimination or consolidation.

Shifts in Authority to State Agencies

Many two-year colleges are organized and controlled by local districts and receive state funds on a formula similar to that for elementary and secondary schools. Others have closer ties to state agencies. When appropriate, public two-year institutions are included in the discussion below. However, attention is largely devoted to public universities and comprehensive institutions. The number of administrators of private institutions responding to the "off-campus" subitems is too small for meaningful analysis.

In the minds of college presidents, do shifts in authority to state agencies coincide with shifts in campus authority relationships? The answer is a qualified "yes" for public doctoral-granting universities and comprehensive colleges and universities (Table 80). A large proportion of those reporting a shift in authority from departments to campus administrators see more power moving from the campus to the governor (71 percent) and the legislature (56 percent). Among the presidents noting a shift in authority from campus administration to departments the comparable numbers are 31 percent (governor) and 36 percent (legislature). Just the opposite pattern, however, appears in the case of campus authority and the coordinating agency. Those presidents noting a decrease in the shift of power from departments to campus administrators (53 percent) are more likely than those mentioning increases (38 percent) to report that authority on campus has given way to coordinating agencies. Even this exception fails to hold when it comes to the period 1974–1980 (Table 80).

A larger proportion of presidents of public universities and comprehensive colleges than of other types of institutions report shifts in authority from boards to coordinating agencies, the state executive, and the legislature. (See Table 19; compare

Table 19. Shift in general decision-making authority from governing board to various state offices reported by public senior colleges and universities,[a] 1968–1974 (in percentages of responding institutions)

	Shift in authority from governing board to		
		State budget	
	Coordinating	& finance	State
Extent of shift	agency	(governor)	legislature
	(N = 187)	(N = 239)	(N = 237)
Increased	48	51	39
Same or decreased	52	49	61

[a]Research universities, doctoral universities, comprehensive colleges and universities, and liberal arts colleges.

with averages in Appendix A, Question 38.) The difference is especially great for coordinating agencies. The relatively low proportion of respondents noting a shift in power to the legislature comes as some surprise, since legislatures during the past three years have begun staffing their principal appropriations and finance committees with professional personnel who take a very active role in the review of budgets and the analysis of productivity and accountability.[2] There may be considerable

[2]See *State budgeting for higher education: Data Digest* (1975). Center for Research and Development in Higher Education.

lag-time between such activity and the respondents' awareness of it. Or, it may be that the administrators know what is going on but attach relatively little significance to it at this time.

One reason often given by state political leaders for assuming authority over public institutions is that higher education fails to respond to the needs of students and society without prodding, planning, and initiative from the state level.[3] Indeed, increased authority for the governor (and to a lesser extent the legislature) has a greater positive relationship to new programs for ethnic minorities than does a shift in authority to the co-ordinating agency (Table 81). This result is not surprising, given the political pressures and conflicts that arose over such programs in the late 1960s. On the other hand, it seems that increased authority for the state legislature has a negative relationship to programs designed for evening students. This may result from the traditional reluctance of legislatures to appropriate the additional money to fund adult and part-time students on the same basis as regular students, for surely the idea of using campuses for more hours of the day remains a popular idea with political leaders.

One claim sometimes advanced by administrators of public institutions is that they cannot be responsive to needs arising from changing social conditions because state agencies exercise close control over administrative and policy decisions. Preaudits, appropriations riders, ceilings on reserves and carryovers, position control, and other techniques are said to limit the freedom of institutional leaders to make major changes in program and operations.

Presidents of public institutions did see a decrease between 1968 and 1974 in flexibility in campus use of funds from state government, which paralleled a shift in authority to state agencies. To illustrate, presidents who report a shift in power

[3]Eventually, some political leaders may have second thoughts about such arguments if institutions actively recruit new adult constituencies and expect the state to fund them at rates for regular students. As discussed in Chapter 5, over half the presidents report an "increase" between 1968 and 1974 in the number of instructional programs designed to serve four types of "new students."

to the governor's office are considerably more likely than other presidents to feel that they have less flexibility at the campus level in use of state funds (Table 82). The same relationship holds but is slightly weaker in the case of shifts in authority to coordinating agencies and legislatures.

We have already discussed in some detail change in the use of various planning and management techniques (see Chapter 6). With few exceptions there is little correlation between presidential perceptions of shifts in authority to state agencies and the extent of change in the use of selected management tools (Table 83). The exceptions, however, are noteworthy. Of the presidents of public universities and comprehensive colleges experiencing a loss of authority to coordinating agencies, 45 percent report extensive change in the use of management information systems (MIS). The comparable proportion of those not reporting such a loss is 32 percent. Similarly, a much larger fraction of presidents report an extensive change in use of faculty workload studies when authority is seen as having shifted to the legislature (41 percent) than when it has not (32 percent). Regarding both branches of state government and coordinating agencies, a change in campus use of WICHE-NCHEMS products is greater if power has shifted to each of these bodies than if it has not.

Perhaps we should note in passing that we have also examined perceived shifts in general decision-making authority to state agencies in relation to a number of other variables, including changes in: (1) state funds, (2) number of faculty and administrators, (3) FTE enrollment, and (4) program or course consolidation. We have, however, found practically no differences of any magnitude.

Master Plans

Long-range, comprehensive planning came into vogue for higher education during the great enrollment expansion of the 1960s. Most institutions developed plans for campus buildings. Some institutions planned the academic programs to be housed in them. Systems officers supported plans to establish building priorities, to aid resource allocation and to keep campuses from unnecessary duplication of program efforts. State coordinating agencies created statewide plans for much the same reasons, but also to lay out the roles and functions of sets of campuses, systems, and segments. By the end of the 1960s almost every institution, system, and state government had some instrument or series of instruments that could be labeled a "master plan."

The vast majority of administrators (86 percent) report that institutional plans have helped their institutions over the years since 1968 (see Appendix A, Question 37). Comparable percentages of those responding to our queries regarding system and statewide plans are 58 and 47 percent—with another 11 and 16 percent, respectively, saying that such plans hindered their institutions. It is worth recalling that our survey measures the perceptions of presidents and their staffs, not those of faculty, students, citizen groups, political leaders, or state-agency personnel, many of whom would doubtless have a somewhat different view of whether a plan had "helped," "hindered," or had "no effect" on an institution of higher education.

Are presidents of independent senior public institutions more likely than presidents of institutions within systems to feel that institutional master plans have "helped"? The answer is a bit surprising (Table 84). A greater percentage of institutions within systems had plans between 1968 and 1974: 85 versus 75 percent for independent campuses. Of those with plans, nearly identical proportions of presidents say that the plans have helped their institutions: 83 percent of those within systems; 85 percent of those standing alone.

It may well be that the admonition often given in the past by state-level planners to institutional officers is given to officers at the system level as well: "Either do a good job of planning for the institution or we will do it for you." By creating its own plan the institution may, in effect, force system (and state-level) planners to take less initiative and to adopt the institution's objectives and goals. In these circumstances, institutional plans would be viewed by the presidents as of great help, which they apparently are.

The relationship between master planning and changes in enrollment may not be apparent. Institutional plans may call for emphasis on particular levels or types of programs (for example, occupational, graduate, lower-division) or on special services, such as counseling or housing, and thus attract clientele who might not otherwise have enrolled. At the state level, master plans frequently place ceilings on enrollments of lower-division students in senior institutions to direct the flow of students toward community colleges. Some state plans limit graduate programs to one or more institutions. Furthermore, special grant programs may be inaugurated to aid students in attending private institutions. California, Florida, and Illinois are good examples of states that have used most of these devices to redirect the flow of students.

Compared to those who indicate that statewide master plans had no effect, or had hindered their institution, a larger proportion of presidents who see a statewide master plan as having helped report FTE enrollment increases of more than 10 percent between 1968 and 1974 (Table 85). This pattern holds for each type of institution shown. Basically the same pattern holds for perceptions of the effect of institutional plans (Table 86). While it is likely that presidents in growing institutions are more likely to report that such plans help, the plans themselves may facilitate institutional growth.

Since statewide master plans call for data on institutional costs and programs, such plans might be expected to influence the use of various management techniques. We shall briefly discuss here the relationship with MIS. The results are similar for other management techniques. Both for senior colleges and universities and public two-year institutions, presidents reporting that state plans helped are more likely than those reporting that state plans had no effect to have made extensive changes in the use of MIS between 1968 and 1974 (Table 87). At the same time, presidents of public institutions who say state plans hindered them are even more likely than those who feel they were helped to have made extensive changes in MIS usage. The pattern to 1980 is basically the same.

Regional and State Variation

Perceptions of shifts in authority vary by state. Presidents of public universities and comprehensive colleges in only five states

(California, Illinois, New York, Pennsylvania, and Wisconsin) account for 45 percent of the total across the country who report shifts in authority from departments to campus administrators. Presidents of other senior public institutions in these same states account for only 15 percent of the total number reporting shifts in the other direction (Table 20). Each of the five states has one or more systems of public institutions with numerous campuses operating under one or more governing boards and central administrations. Presidents of private institutions in these states, on the other hand, are about evenly distributed between having seen increases and decreases in shifts in authority from departments to campus administration.

Perceived shifts in authority from campus governing bodies to state agencies is less concentrated—at least by major region of the country (Table 88). Among officials of public senior institutions, those in the Great Lakes/Plains and Southeast regions are more likely than those in the North Atlantic and West/Southwest to see a shift in power toward coordinating agencies. Officials of senior public institutions in the Great

Table 20. Percentages in five selected states of senior institutions[a] reporting increases and decreases in the shift of general decision-making authority from department to campus administration, 1968–1974, by control

State	Public			Private		
	Increase campus admin.	*Decrease campus admin.*	*Total*	*Increase campus admin.*	*Decrease campus admin.*	*Total*
Total, all states	(N = 54)	(N = 53)	(N = 234)	(N = 29)	(N = 27)	(N = 115)
Percentage located in						
California	18	4	8	b	b	4
Illinois	6	2	3	b	4	4
New York	9	2	6	17	26	16
Pennsylvania	6	2	4	3	4	9
Wisconsin	6	6	4	3	b	2
Total percentage in five states	45	15	25	24	33	35

[a]Research universities, doctoral universities, and comprehensive colleges and universities.
[b]No observations.

Lakes/Plains region are also more likely than others to mention a shift in authority to the state executive. A disproportionate number in the Southeast see authority moving away from the governor, the reason for which may be the growing influence of coordinating agencies in southern states. Finally, presidents in the Great Lakes/Plains and West/Southwest are more likely than their counterparts elsewhere to perceive a shift in authority toward the legislature. Again, presidents of senior public institutions in the Southeast are more likely to report a "decrease" in the shift of authority to legislatures.

With respect to statewide master plans, more administrators of four-year institutions in the Great Lakes/Plains region than elsewhere say such plans have hindered their institutions (Table 89). This is not surprising, since many presidents in this area see a shift in power from the campus to all three agencies of state government. Part of their disappointment in state plans may be tied to the growth of two-year institutions, since presidents of these latter institutions in the Great Lakes/Plains region are more likely than their counterparts elsewhere to report that statewide plans have helped them.

To ascertain how state master plans in some of the larger states are viewed, we have examined those states in our survey in which 15 or more institutions reported having such plans. The resulting 12 states are ranked in Table 90 by number of responding institutions. Since the overall response rate to our questionnaire was only 50 percent, the pattern in Table 90 may not accurately reflect the true pattern in each state.

The 12 states contain nearly two-thirds of the presidents in the entire survey who report state plans as either helping or hindering their institutions. State plans, of course, tend to assign resources and program priorities to some institutions and not others. For example, the New York state master plan calls for substantial subsidies to private institutions. Authority to award the Ph.D. degree is restricted in several states to a few institutions. And in some states, the community colleges are much favored in new construction and funding over the senior public institutions. Thus, there may be good reasons for individual presidents to state that plans hindered rather than helped their institutions. Such a statement does not mean a plan is bad. On the contrary, the plan may be the best means of optimizing use of limited state resources. One should not draw hasty conclusions about the quality of state plans from our data. Much more information for each state is needed to make an assessment.

Presidents in New York and Oklahoma are more likely than presidents in the other states to say that their state plan has helped rather than hindered their institution. The pattern in New York is especially noteworthy, since over half the respondents there head private colleges and universities. We suspect that in New York abundant student aid and efforts to assist private colleges account for this response pattern. Only in Maryland does the ratio of "helped" responses to the "hindered" responses drop below the *average* of the 38 states not shown. Finally, we wish to point out that of the 12 states, only two have no state coordinating agency—Kansas and North Carolina. North Carolina had such an agency until 1972. It had completed statewide plans prior to being superseded by a single governing board for all public universities and colleges. The evidence presented here supports observations made by Berdahl (1971), Glenny et al. (1971), and other researchers that state planning is most extensive in states where coordinating agencies rather than single governing boards are found. Today, 27 states have coordinating agencies, 10 of which show up among the 12 states listed. There are 19 statewide governing boards for public senior-level institutions (some also cover two-year institutions), of which only two fall into this group of twelve.

8

Impact of the Leveling of Enrollment and Funding on Quality of Students, Programs, and Faculty

If stable or declining enrollments and funding had only benign effects, there would be little concern about so-called steady state conditions. There is reason to believe, however, that while the adjustments necessitated by the "new realities" of financial stringency and stable enrollments may be beneficial in some ways, they are likely to be deleterious in others.

To learn what presidents see as some of the ramifications of the new conditions for their institutions, we asked:

Does the leveling of enrollment and funding enhance or impair the quality of:
a. students?   __enhances   __impairs
   (please explain)
b. faculty?   __enhances   __impairs
   (please explain)
c. programs?   __enhances   __impairs
   (please explain)

Not all administrators responded. Of the three-quarters who did, some refused to be constrained by the choice of either "enhances" or "impairs." A few presidents indicated that both effects are likely or that they didn't know what effect the changes have had or will have. A much larger number suggested that declining growth has had neither a positive nor a negative effect. These officials used such terms as "no effect," "no change," and "none."

Before describing the pattern of responses in detail, a few preliminary remarks are in order. First of all, we made no attempt to define the term "quality" in the survey instrument. In a few instances, what would appear to be identical consequences have been judged differently. Second, because presidents often emphasize different aspects (or dimensions) of fairly global influences such as the economy, student demand for college degrees, the draft, and the like, they sometimes differ in their opinions of the "net" effect on quality. This problem is not simply one of selective perception. The relative impact of divergent forces varies from one institution to another. Consider, for example, the quality of students. If a declining proportion of young people choose to go to college, some institutions may accept students who otherwise would not attend any institution. But if those who do attend are, on balance, more motivated than students in past years, one can easily see how two presidents— both faced with enrollment problems—might respond differently to the quality question. Even if both administrators defined "quality" in terms of academic aptitude and motivation, the strength of these countervailing influences might well differ.

We begin the rest of this chapter with a statistical description of the responses to the three parts of the quality question. We examine interrelationships among the three and relative differences as they relate to: (1) selected institutional characteristics (for example, Carnegie typology, control, and location), and (2) reported changes in enrollments and funding (that is, expenditures per FTE student). We then examine the narrative responses concerning student quality in the second section of the chapter and point to additional correlates of enhance-impair responses. The third and fourth sections take up, in turn, effects of steady state on programs and faculty.

Overall Pattern of Responses

Compared to those who say that the quality of students and programs is enhanced by a leveling of enrollment and funding over one and one-half as many presidents feel that their quality is impaired (Table 21). Perceptions of negative effects outweigh perceptions of positive ones for quality of faculty, too, but the

Table 21. Perceived effect of leveling of enrollment and funding on quality of students, programs, and faculty, 1974 (in percentages of responding institutions)

Effect	Students	Programs	Faculty
	(N = 941)	(N = 933)	(N = 952)
Enhances	29	32	38
Impairs	45	54	44
Neither	21	9	12
Both	1	2	2
Don't know	4	3	4

ratio is much smaller—approximately 12 to 10.

Presidents of private institutions are considerably more likely than their public-institution counterparts to see adverse effects on the quality of students (Table 91).[1] The presidents of private research and other doctoral-granting universities are especially concerned about the quality of students—with representatives of private liberal arts and two-year institutions only slightly less so. Private universities have traditionally been quite selective in admissions. This may account for part of the difference. Among public institutions, only in comprehensive institutions does the number of officials reporting impaired student quality exceed the number reporting enhanced quality by a wide margin: two to one. Indeed, more representatives of

[1]Furthermore, among four-year institutions, proportionately more presidents of independent private colleges than religiously affiliated ones see a deterioration in student quality (table not shown).

public two-year institutions say that stable enrollments and funding "enhance" than say they "impair" the quality of students. Student quality in some of these schools is related to former draft-induced enrollments, and the presence of better-motivated students today.

The number of presidents of public four-year colleges and universities who see impaired programs resulting from steady-state conditions far exceeds the number seeing enhanced programs. Officials in private research universities respond in much the same way. Only in private comprehensive colleges do more presidents mention positive than negative effects on program. Their reasons, discussed in detail later in the chapter, generally reflect the results of what might be called "judicious pruning of dead wood."

Approximately equal numbers of officials of private institutions see enhanced and impaired effects of steady-state conditions on the quality of faculty, but there are major differences by type of institution. "Faculty impairment" is the dominant response of leaders of private research and other doctoral-granting institutions. In other categories, about the same number see positive as see negative effects. In public two-year institutions the number saying "enhanced" faculty quality is nearly equal to the number saying "impaired" quality. Again, presidents of public four-year colleges and universities are more pessimistic than their private-institution colleagues.

College officials in some locations are more likely than those in others to see leveling enrollment or funding as having adverse effects (Table 92). Presidents of two-year institutions, both public and private, that are located in small towns or rural areas are more likely than their urban counterparts to report adverse effects on the quality of students, programs, and faculty. Public four- or five-year colleges, on the other hand, display the reverse pattern; more presidents in large urban areas than elsewhere report impaired quality in programs (80 percent) and faculty (67 percent). (However, the number of public urban colleges among our respondents—about 20—is quite small.) Administrators of public universities in "other urban" or in "small town, rural" areas are more likely than their counterparts in large urban areas to see negative impacts on students, programs, and faculty. The picture for private universities, on the other hand, is mixed. Those outside large urban areas are inclined to report adverse effects on students and programs; their urban counterparts are more likely to see a negative impact on faculty.

Presidents generally agree that if one dimension of quality (students, programs, or faculty) is affected by steady state conditions, the other dimensions are affected in a similar way. In public universities and comprehensive colleges, for example, of those officials who feel that the quality of students is impaired in such conditions, about three-fourths see a similar effect on faculty, and an even higher proportion (88 percent) hold the same view concerning program (Table 93). While the degree of association varies, basically the same pattern prevails among other kinds of institutions, both public and private.

Thus far, we have not distinguished between the views of administrators who have actually experienced a leveling of enrollment or funding and those who have not. Clearly, the views of the former are based more on reality than those of the latter. Within the public sector there are sufficient sample cases of those who have experienced steady-state conditions, and of those who have not, to say something about the views of officials both in four-year institutions (exclusive of liberal arts colleges) and in two-year institutions. Among the public senior colleges and universities, presidents who have actually experienced stable or declining enrollment or funding are more likely than those who have not to report impaired quality of students, programs, and faculty (Tables 94 and 95). The difference is especially striking in the case of faculty quality. Of the presidents reporting no growth in both enrollments and funding, 70 percent say that the quality of faculty has been impaired, while only 19 percent say it has been enhanced. Among public two-year institutions, differences in perceived effects are much smaller. Presidents of the relatively few two-year institutions that report stable or declining enrollments and funding are more likely than presidents of other two-year institutions to say that the quality of faculty has been adversely affected; but they are inclined to find the quality of students enhanced.

Turning to the private sector we can comment on the liberal arts colleges separately from other four-year institutions. Representatives of liberal arts colleges that experienced little change in enrollments between 1968 and 1974 are more likely than growing colleges to say the quality of students, programs, and faculty has worsened. Those experiencing actual decreases in enrollment are even more likely to respond in this way. Of the other senior institutions in the private sector, "no growth" in the number of dollars expended per FTE student is related to a perceived impairment of student quality; "no growth" in enrollment is related to perceptions of adverse changes in the quality of faculty.

Impact on Student Quality

One in five administrators asserts that so-called steady-state conditions neither "enhance" nor "impair" the quality of students. In a typical response, the administrator of a comprehensive university with stable enrollments says: "So far no discernible effects. Factors causing declines apparently have offsetting effects." As reported earlier in the chapter, however, 45 percent of the presidents indicate that the quality of students has been (or will be) impaired; only 29 percent say it will be enhanced.

Although we shall focus on the reasons that presidents report student quality will be impaired, a few words should be said about the thinking of those who report that steady-state conditions positively affect the quality of students. A common attitude is that students who do choose to attend college are more highly motivated than in the past. One president reports: "The uninterested don't enroll." Another says: "Only those who want to come, come." And another states: "Students are more motivated." One administrator attributes an increase in improvement in his institution's retention rate to improved student quality. In several cases, officials see a positive effect from faculty members' being able to spend more time with each student. There is no relationship, however, between perceived effects on student quality and changes in faculty teaching load (contact hours) between 1968 and 1974 (table not shown). Of course, contact hours are generally thought of in terms of time spent with students in the classroom. With slipping enrollments, some faculty members may be trying to correct the condition by spending more time with students outside of class.

Turning to perceptions of the negative effects of steady-state conditions, presidents frequently mention less selectivity in admissions as a major reason for reduced quality of students. As we pointed out in Chapter 5, the extent of modifications of admissions standards over the past six years is related to stable or declining enrollments, at least to some extent. Among senior institutions, both public and private, administrators who report "extensive" or "some" change in admissions standards between 1968 and 1974 are more likely than those reporting "very little" change to mention that a leveling of enrollments and funding impairs student quality (Table 96). An important interaction effect involving a third variable, however, is apparent. Specifically, of the presidents of four-year institutions who report extensive or some change in admissions standards, those who experienced an increase in FTE enrollments are more likely than those who did not to feel that student quality has been impaired. The opposite pattern prevails among senior institutions that made very little change in admissions standards. Presidents of such no-growth institutions are more likely than those of growing institutions to say that student quality has been impaired. There are at least three possible reasons for this. First, these no-growth institutions have actually experienced the leveling and have a better basis for judgment. Second, while institutions may report little change in admissions standards, steady or declining enrollment may mean that many have a smaller pool of applicants from which to choose. And even though *standards* have not changed, administrators may feel that their institutions are not as selective. Finally, as we indicated in Chapter 2, many of these institutions were already pursuing an open admissions policy back in the late 1960s.

In three out of four instances where we have a sufficient number of observations to permit a meaningful comparison, stable or decreased expenditure per student is correlated with a greater chance of reported impairment than reported enhancement in institutions which have modified their undergraduate admission standards (Table 97). Among the senior institutions administrators are more likely to report that student quality is impaired where admissions standards have been modified, and in the public institutions also where expenditures per student have stabilized or decreased. Only among private senior institutions is the reported change in student quality unrelated to dollars expended per FTE student.

Some presidents see reduced funding as hampering their ability to recruit the "better" student. One private college official notes: "The loss of adequate funding forces colleges toward admission of any student who can pay, and limits the funds available for aid to the best students. . . ." Some institutions report a greater tendency to admit "high risk" students. Others think the quality of their students is impaired because they cannot recruit as they would like to do, from a lack of funds. One president says, "We are relatively unable to go after the 'special' students (the very bright, handicapped, ethnic, poverty-level, etc.) because resources are utilized so as to be maximally efficient; for example, in recruitment we go where we can count on good contacts. We can't afford to meander around looking for isolated cases." High tuition and limited scholarship funding "exclude many good quality students," reports the administrator of a private university.

How common are these "recruitment effects"? We find practically no association between perceived changes in student quality and changes in emphasis on recruitment of traditional students between 1968 and 1974. For that matter, there is very little relationship between perceived changes in student quality and changed emphasis on recruitment of transfer students, ethnic minorities, low-income, or evening students. On the other hand, those who stepped up their recruitment of early admissions from high school, adults, and off-campus students are more likely than average to report impairment in the quality of students, at least in the case of public four-year institutions (Table 98).

For several reasons, we are reluctant to draw any cause-effect conclusions from these responses. First, early admissions from high school are often honors students, and several studies reveal that adults in college are typically of high quality in terms of achievement, motivation, and academic ability. Second, among public institutions that have experienced little change or a decrease in enrollments, recruitment of off-campus students is positively related to enhancement of student quality. In sum, the data are inconclusive regarding recruitment efforts and changes in the quality of students.

Aside from modifications of admissions standards and changes in the mix of students (for example, traditional versus adult), the effect of the steady state on student quality may be mediated, in some cases, by changes in the number of programs. Controlling for change in FTE enrollment from 1968 to 1974, the relationship between changes in number of undergraduate programs and perceptions of student quality is, however, unclear at best. There is no relationship between these two variables in: (1) public four-year institutions that increased in enrollment from 1968 to 1974, (2) private four-year institutions that had steady or declining enrollment, and (3) expanding public two-year colleges (table not shown). On the other hand, for public senior colleges and universities with no enrollment growth between 1968 and 1974, institutions that increased their undergraduate programs are more likely to report enhanced student quality and less likely to report impairment than those that did not increase their offerings (Table 99). The opposite pattern holds for private four-year institutions with enrollment increases.

As pointed out in Chapter 5, the questionnaire item concerning change in the number of instructional programs for "new students" fails to distinguish between creation of a new program and making existing curricula available to new clientele by rescheduling, taking professors off campus, and the like. Thus, while for most institutions there is practically no relationship between changes in the number of programs for "new students" and perceived effects of the steady state on student quality, the pattern for public four-year institutions follows that reported earlier in terms of changing emphasis on recruitment (Table 100). Namely, those institutions reporting little change or a decrease in changes in recruitment are more likely than those who reported an increase to feel that enrollment and funding changes have adversely affected student quality.

Regardless of the lack of consistent relationships in perceived changes in student quality and changes in the number of programs, it is perhaps worth noting one president's thinking on the matter: "While no quantitative measure of student quality has changed, curriculum offerings are reduced, which means that the better student will be less interested in enrolling."

Impact on Program Quality

A majority (54 percent) of the nearly 1,000 administrators who answered the question on the effects of leveling of enrollments and funding on the quality of programs report negative effects. One-third, however, say that programs are enhanced. The reason most often cited for program improvement is increased efficiency. One president says: "A lot less garbage." Another put it this way: "Some of the 'fat' has been removed. . . ." Similar comments are:

> We're being forced to prune out somewhat and to be more imaginative. I believe the year to come will show us stronger and more creative for having had to tighten our belts.
>
> We are reinforcing strengths, planning expansion which seems warranted by demands, and pruning judiciously.
>
> Financial stress dictates more and sharper efforts for effective programs.
>
> Competition for students will tax the ingenuity of faculty and administration to provide programs that are relevant to the student.

According to some officials, leveling stimulates innovation. But, as pointed out in Chapter 5, while we cannot be certain of the direction of causal influence, an increase in the number of instructional programs is related more to enrollment growth than to stagnation. Competitive pressures may induce some innovations *within* existing programs that would not otherwise occur. As we shall see in a moment, however, a leveling of funding is often seen by college and university presidents as impairing the quality of programs precisely because new money facilitates innovative activity. Some presidents foresee better service to fewer students. One official puts it this way: "Since there is little, if any, overcrowding of students in most programs, those students who enroll can be served better."

Of those who state that the quality of programs is impaired by steady-state conditions, arguments center on four implications. First, less money and fewer students generally means some decrease in the number of faculty and, therefore, reduction in course and program offerings. Second, expenditures on equipment, books, and related support services may have to be cut. Third, less money may be available for course development, experimentation, and program innovation. Fourth, some presidents note the great difficulty of reallocating existing resources. Other reasons include morale problems and inflation.

The following observations are rather typical of those who argue, in effect, that "fewer programs means poorer programs."

. . . more limited course offerings.

Since student enrollments have decreased by approximately 20 percent in the last five years, the result has been a lessening of the number of curricular choices offered to students.

Not all desirable programs can be supported.

Some programs, good for the college to offer, will need to be eliminated.

Programs will have less breadth and depth due to lack of highly specialized faculty members.

Legislatures still are playing the numbers game. Loss of enrollment means a cut in funding. Any cut in funding results in a cut in services.

With regard to equipment, books, and enrichment activities, administrators have this to say:

There is less opportunity for enriching departmental offerings . . . providing equipment, etc.

Unable to provide new educational equipment [and] facilities or [to] respond to new student and faculty interests.

Equipment not replaced, library not expanded.

No funds for . . . ongoing faculty workshops and seminars.

We noted in Chapter 5 that the leveling of enrollment and funding can both spur and retard innovation. Judging from the remarks of our respondents, adverse consequences are uppermost in the minds of presidents who comment on this matter:

Insufficient funds to develop new programs to meet needs of students.

Lower levels of funding inhibit the initiation of additional programs for which there may be a market.

No funds for course development.

Lack of funding produces fewer "experiments" in educational programs and therefore a more static curriculum.

"Risk" funds for new programs not available.

Several presidents reason that the quality of programs is impaired because of difficulties experienced in reallocating resources from one program to another:

Because of lack of flexibility in shifting both fund sources and faculty resources.

. . . limited funding can permit new programs if old moribund ones are dropped.

Difficult to shift resources to match changing needs.

If some programs can only be strengthened at the detriment of other programs, I am not certain that we will be able to muster the courage to eliminate some of our programs.

Our problem with leveling enrollment will be to retool the present faculty so they are more versatile.

Faculty are not as ready to move to new locations, so we have staff who cannot teach in new curricular areas. Without new staff skills, we are hindered in developing new programs.

Impact on Faculty Quality

Thus, the effects of leveling enrollment and funding on programs and faculty are often intertwined. Nearly as many presidents say that the quality of faculty is enhanced as say it is impaired: 38 and 45 percent, respectively.

Two major themes run through the comments on positive effects on faculty. First, because of a large pool of well-qualified candidates, institutions are able to be selective in hiring faculty. Typical comments are:

It's currently a buyer's market.

The number of people seeking faculty status is increasing for the number of jobs available; hence the choice becomes greater. Competition for jobs seems to necessitate better preparation for applicants.

The second reason involves winnowing of poorer quality faculty and efforts to upgrade the performance of those who remain:

We reduce the quantity of dead wood and are more careful in selection of new faculty. Systematic evaluation of effectiveness is wired to salary and promotion.

The weak are destroyed.

Possibly permits more critical evaluation of professional performance in a period of financial stress.

Presidents who say that faculty quality is impaired cite a number of reasons, including a lack of funds necessary to turn a buyer's market to best advantage:

Even though there is a buyer's market in the academic world, there will not be funds available to employ experienced faculty with exceptional credentials.

[Faculty] development efforts are also adversely affected by leveling of funds.

The compensation issue is uppermost in the minds of many respondents, especially in institutions where funding has leveled off:

Cannot pay adequate salaries, cannot retain excellent faculty. Tighter budgets may affect salary increments and other inducements such as a lighter teaching load.

Can't buy quality faculty.

Compensation likely to fall below competitive levels.

Insufficient funds.

Even if untenured faculty are not forced to go, they may leave in search of greater security:

Capable faculty, particularly the untenured, are tending to seek and accept positions of greater security.

With the fear of retrenchment, the better faculty are the ones with the opportunities for moving.

Some see adverse effects on faculty morale:

Creates a defensive attitude as security decreases.

Faculty morale is adversely affected by lower enrollments and raises that do not keep up with the cost of living.

Affects teaching.

The administrator of a public two-year institution that has had falling enrollments suggests a rather ugly picture in explaining why leveling impairs the quality of faculty: "Staff reduction and program retrenchment creates an atmosphere of apprehension, fear, and distrust."

Increased faculty workload is another reason cited for impairment of faculty quality. As pointed out in Chapter 5, approximately one-third of our respondents say that they are planning a change in the student-faculty ratio. Most expect the ratio to rise. With increased enrollments and decreased dollars per student, one president reports: "Faculty loads are by far the heaviest of any state institution." Another factor mentioned by presidents is inflexibility stemming from an increase in the tenure ratio. One official says, "In a small liberal arts college, there are few programs; hence stagnation tends to set in." Another puts it this way: "We are locked into existing faculty—no free flow—everyone comes up for tenure—no youth."

Other, more complex comments on faculty quality include the following:

Since the economic crunch and enrollment fall-off is national, the academic market is glutted with available faculty. On the other hand, with increased workloads and decreased real salaries, this is a short-term benefit and will become a liability in the long term.

The most difficult challenge facing any institution is to stimulate faculty productivity and to develop a high sense of faculty morale so that faculty members do want to do a better job regardless of the number of students they have.

On the one hand, there is always the possibility of increasing turnover among faculty and of obtaining even better qualified faculty members in a tight job market. On the other hand, there is always the problem of internal pressures to force the institution to take on the responsibility of retraining and retooling faculty members who cannot perform in areas where they are needed. Most faculties will not on their own undertake any rigorous self-development program, and this requirement therefore falls on the shoulders of the chief administrative officers.

9

Policy, Practice, and the Broader Context

In this chapter, we consider administrators' observations within the broader social context, identify policy issues, and raise questions that, we hope, will help clarify opportunities and constraints.

The aggregation of responses of the individual presidents yields a basically optimistic set of views. Fewer see growth in total enrollments in the future (1974–1980) than saw them in the past (1968–1974), but fewer also see declines. Many expect to solve present enrollment difficulties by attracting adult, off-campus, and evening students. Funding problems do not dominate the views of administrators in our survey. Growth remains the expectation—not decline. Presidents hope to tap alumni, corporations, foundations, and other private sources for more funds than in the past. Although they are aware of difficulties brought on by current conditions, most presidents express confidence in the ability of their institutions to modify curricular offerings, to reallocate resources where needed, and to otherwise plan and manage wisely the resources available to them. No major changes are foreseen. Rather, recent changes are projected as meeting institutional and student needs of the future.

In this chapter, we focus on some of the interrelationships and dilemmas not always evident in the topic-by-topic presentation of material in the body of the report. We consider:

(1) broad societal trends, (2) important external conditions (for example, inflation, recession), and (3) policy dilemmas that appear problematic to us. We hope that this discussion of issues will provide a more realistic basis for social policy and institutional practice.

The Search for New Clientele

A major goal of the vast majority of institutions is to maintain or increase enrollments. While continuing to emphasize programs for traditional students, most presidents expect their institutions to recruit a wide range of nontraditional students as well—adults, part-time evening students, persons off-campus, and those principally interested in continuing education. Several difficulties, however, are clear:

- Few presidents see much expansion in personnel assigned to the function of recruitment and admissions.
- The untapped pool of adults may not be large enough to meet the enrollment aspirations of all institutions. Although a number of rather traditional, four-year institutions have been successful in attracting adults to selected programs, many colleges are in small towns and rural areas and, thus, poorly situated to serve this new market. Then, too, the proportion of adults interested in degree programs as opposed to noncredit courses may not be very large.
- Continuing education services in most states must be self-supporting, except at the community college level. Altering this practice will not be easy. Yet, without full financing of adult programs, it may be difficult to attract large numbers of new students.
- Many institutions may not be in a position to develop occupational and professional programs for young people, who have been shifting away from liberal arts to more vocationally oriented programs. Nor will it be easy to respond to the particular learning needs of adults. Adults have not, in the past, attended degree-credit programs in large numbers. Nor do they express much interest in traditional liberal arts programs. Rather, they typically seek learning experiences—at

convenient times and places—that will help them in meeting everyday problems in their lives. Nevertheless, responses of the presidents imply that many institutions will seek to offer "old wine in new bottles." Moreover, those intent on building new curricula may not have the capital needed to do so, or will need to dig development money out of regular operating funds.

- For some areas of study (for example, business administration), the market for adult students appears destined to become glutted with new offerings. If adult education is subsidized, some uneconomical programs may result. If self-supporting, some colleges and universities will surely end up losing money in the unbridled competition for the same student groups.

- Oversupplies of trained persons will surely develop in a number of currently popular technical and quasi-professional areas. As happened in the case of teachers and Ph.D.s, students and the public may become disenchanted with higher education if the labor market is unable to absorb graduates into training-related occupations.

- Will the right people be available to teach in new programs, at new times and places? Presidents foresee nontenured and part-time faculty bearing the brunt of reductions in staff. This pattern runs counter to traditions in staffing for part-time, adult students. Moreover, on campus, faculty are not easily shifted from one discipline to another, and there is little precedent (or money) for retraining them.

- Presidents anticipate more collective bargaining in the future than in the past. Indeed, they may well encourage collective bargaining by instituting teacher evaluation, higher promotion and tenure standards, and heavier workloads. While collective agreements may add to flexibility in some ways (for example, perhaps retraining and early retirement programs), such agreements are more likely to inhibit it in others (for example, restrictions on time and place of instruction, workload definitions and amounts, rates of pay for moonlighting).

Securing Adequate Resources

We have already noted the problem of securing funds for special purposes, such as program development and faculty retraining. Equally serious is the matter of rising unit costs and dwindling funds—and, consequently, declining services—as enrollments fall and wages and prices go up. Despite present problems, most presidents expect a higher level of funding from their traditional sources in 1980 than they receive today. Alumni, corporations, foundations, continuing education programs, and state government are seen as increasingly important. To meet rising costs and maintain and improve services, presidents face a number of problems:

- At the time of the survey (summer 1974), inflation was a serious problem. The market value of investment portfolios had declined. Endowment incomes had fallen some. Several foundations had announced cutting back grants; others were quietly doing so. Few foundations now wish to deplete their capital to maintain current levels of support for higher education. Special appeals for instructional funds are likely to fall on deaf ears if graduates continue to have difficulty finding employment in their chosen fields.
- For most states, revenues have fallen off as a consequence of the economic recession. More important in the long run, even prior to the recession three-quarters of the states (including all of the large industrial ones) allocated a smaller share of their general revenues to higher education in 1973 than in immediately preceding years (Glenny and Kidder, 1974). State revenue increases and state surpluses in recent years have not generally gone to colleges and universities. At both state and national levels, budget analysts and political leaders place higher education services toward the low end of the priority listing of essential social services.
- Some private colleges expect to "go public" in order to increase their funding base and ward off threats to their survival. As enrollments drop in some public institutions, it is likely to become increasingly difficult to justify state support

of private colleges, much less assume full responsibility for them.

- We have already questioned the size of the pool of adult students, which in turn leads us to wonder about the amount of likely additional funding support from adult education. Some universities and a few colleges have long earned substantial amounts of money by offering evening courses on and off campus. The surplus income earned has been used to support other, more costly, "regular" programs. With more institutions of all types offering continuing education programs, the profitability of such efforts may decline.

- Public subsidy for adult degree programs and for off-campus and noncredit work raises a number of complex issues. Historically, most adults have paid the full direct cost of such instructional services. States have subsidized such instruction only if the person attended regular credit classes on campus. States now vary in their treatment of programs for adults. Given problems of energy conservation, urban decay, mass transit, and health and welfare, will citizens seek public support for continued and recurrent education? If full subsidies are voted, will they lead to trouble for private universities and some colleges that count on income from adults? Would equal state subsidies for adult instruction—regardless of its location and its degree-credit or non-degree credit nature—lead to increased costs through elimination of "overload" salary arrangements for regular faculty and the use of part-time and adjunct faculty?

Flexibility, Responsiveness, and Efficiency

Some observers suspect that many four-year institutions, no matter what they do, will be unable to ride out the storm of lower attendance rates and the underlying shift in the age distribution of the population. Other institutions may survive and maintain their vigor through internal efforts to remain flexible and efficient.

- Some presidents report that their institutions have taken expedient and time-honored actions to: (1) consolidate courses and programs, and (2) increase student-faculty ratios and faculty workloads. The majority, however, report little or no change in these areas. Nor do most presidents anticipate additional efforts in these directions to increase efficiency by 1980.

- In general, presidents say that their institutions have not made extensive changes in the use of planning and management techniques. By 1980, however, many more expect substantial change. Will the use of these tools be a panacea? They surely may help individual and collective decision-making, but faith in their value may well exceed what can be achieved through their use.

- Master plans, like other planning and management tools, are generally viewed positively by administrators. In the past, most plans have guided growth. Will planning processes and documents, especially at system and state levels, continue to be a positive force in this period of reduced growth in enrollments and funding? The presidents reply affirmatively, but depression and competition lead almost inevitably to more state control over use of funds and to less flexibility. State and system master plans will help some institutions, while others will be thwarted in achieving their goals.

- Administrators are naturally reluctant to forecast *radical* change in the structure and functioning of their institutions. Merger, consolidation, and consortia-type arrangements may assist some institutions—especially in urban areas—to provide services that otherwise would be out of their reach. Yet, fewer than one in ten presidents anticipates such action between now and 1980.

Concluding Comments

We have pointed to problems and difficulties within and outside institutions of higher education and have raised a number of questions. Our purpose has been to provide a broad perspective on the difficulties that some institutions now face and that others will confront in the years ahead.

By no means do we feel that stability in enrollment and funding is bad. Many presidents anticipated the trends now affecting higher education and took steps to maintain the vitality of their institutions. Others have moved aggressively to reshape their programs to better fit the aspirations of individuals and the nation's emerging social priorities. Some institutions are in a better position than others to change. Many public community colleges, for example, are rapidly restructuring their services to meet the needs of their constituencies. Others, such as nonselective private liberal arts colleges in rural areas, face great difficulties.

Higher education provides an array of services vital to the well-being of individuals and society. It is this fact, more than any other, that leads us to conclude that despite the manifold problems presented by steady-state conditions, there is much room for optimism. A healthier, more diverse set of institutions and postsecondary educational services will surely emerge in the years ahead. And many of the administrators who were kind enough to respond to our questionnaire will be in the forefront of that movement.

Appendix A

Survey Instrument

---

2 July 1974

Dear President:

Many institutions of higher education are faced with dramatic changes in enrollments and funding. In response to these changes, the Center for Research and Development in Higher Education at Berkeley, under a contract with the Carnegie Council on Policy Studies in Higher Education, is conducting a national survey of institutions of higher education to ascertain how they are responding to actual (or projected) downturns in enrollment and finances. The following questionnaire asks for information on changes in operations since 1968, and from the present to 1980. The questions cover such areas as resource acquisition, program and personnel policies, and management practices.

Our goal is to collect information of mutual utility to the many institutions of postsecondary education across the country and to inform the general public of current trends in this area. We value your recollections and perceptions of these trends and issues; thus, we prefer a quick response from you personally rather than your searching for more precise information not readily at hand. Your responses will be used for statistical purposes and will not be identified by institution without authorization. Findings from the survey will be published by the Carnegie Council in the spring of 1975.

To meet a tight time schedule, we would appreciate your kind cooperation in completing the questionnaire and returning it to us in the enclosed airmail envelope by July 19. We greatly value your professional comments and are grateful for your cooperation in this matter.

With kind regards,

Lyman A. Glenny, Director
Center for Research and Development
   in Higher Education, 5th Floor
University of California

Clark Kerr, Chairman
Carnegie Council on Policy Studies
   in Higher Education, 10th Floor

2150 Shattuck Avenue, Berkeley, California 94704

Title of person completing this form: _____

Office: _____

Institution: _____

SURVEY OF PRESIDENTS' RESPONSE TO CHANGES IN ENROLLMENTS AND FINANCING

In responding to this questionnaire, please indicate to the best of your recollection, understanding, and estimation, the nature of various changes that have taken place at your campus from 1968 to the present, and those that you anticipate in the future. Please do not take the time to look up hard data.

For both time periods, check the one alternative for each item that best describes your perception of the situation.

I. BASIC CHANGES IN ENROLLMENT AND FINANCES

	From 1968 to 1974				From 1974 to 1980			
	Increase more than 10%	*Little change*	*Decrease more than 10%*	*1968–1974 (N)*	*Increase more than 10%*	*Little change*	*Decrease more than 10%*	*1974–1980 (N)*
1. Indicate the extent of increase or decrease in total fall enrollment (undergraduate, graduate, day, evening, full-, part-time) by:								
Headcount	63%	20%	17%	(1,218)	46%	50%	4%	(1,185)
FTE	61	22	17	(1,169)	43	51	6	(1,135)
2. Please specify the percentage your enrollment (headcount) changed between fall 1971 and fall 1973.								
Increased 65%				(1,130)				
3% No change								
Decreased 32%								
3. Indicate shifts in your institution's real operating expenditure per FTE student (constant $ per FTE student; adjusted for inflation) ..	55%	39%	6%	(1,055)	48%	49%	3%	(1,003)

4.

> *Alternative 1. Actual enrollments equalled or exceeded projections made in the late sixties*
> *Alternative 2. Actual enrollments fell short of projections by 1-14%*
> *Alternative 3. Actual enrollments fell short of projections by 15% or more*
> *Alternative 4. No projection made in the late sixties*

Mark the one alternative from above which describes the relationship between actual enrollment and projected enrollment ....

	In 1974			1974 (N)
	1	*2*	*3*	*4*
	41%	34%	15%	10% (1,191)

5. If actual enrollments fell short of projections, what factors account for the difference?

6.

> *Alternative 1. Fund a substantial new building program*
> *Alternative 2. Fund moderate building program and some rehabilitation*
> *Alternative 3. Fund primarily rehabilitation*

Mark the one alternative from above which best describes the availability of funds for capital outlay.

	In 1968			In 1974			In 1980			1968 (N)	1974 (N)	1980 (N)
	1	*2*	*3*	*1*	*2*	*3*	*1*	*2*	*3*			
	53	31	16	18	43	39	10	39	51	(1,122)	(1,145)	(1,114)

II. RESOURCE ACQUISITION

7. For each major function, indicate changes in amount of funds for:

	From 1968 to 1974			From 1974 to 1980			1968–1974 (N)	1974–1980 (N)
	Increase	Little change	Decrease	Increase	Little change	Decrease		
Instruction and departmental research	70%	26%	4%	59%	39%	2%	(1,187)	(1,157)
Sponsored research	26	63	11	24	69	7	(962)	(963)
Public service	46	49	5	46	51	3	(1,106)	(1,088)
Academic support (library, TV, etc.)	73	21	6	59	37	4	(1,208)	(1,172)
Student services	70	25	5	49	46	5	(1,202)	(1,171)
Other institutional support (physical plant, etc.)	64	29	7	49	45	6	(1,192)	(1,162)

8. For each funding source, indicate change in financial support:

	1974 compared to 1968			1980 compared to 1974				1968–1974 (N)	1974–1980 (N)
	More	Little change	Less	More	Little change	Less	Not applicable		
Local government	31%	57%	12%	30%	60%	10%		(506)	(505)
State government	78	18	4	70	27	3		(991)	(976)
Federal government	51	31	18	43	45	12		(1,081)	(1,055)
Endowment	42	53	5	60	37	3		(874)	(874)
Foundations & corporations	47	49	4	57	41	2		(984)	(977)
Private donors (including alumni)	60	37	3	72	27	1		(1,031)	(1,018)

| | 1974 compared to 1968 | | | 1980 compared to 1974 | | | | | |
	More	Little change	Less	More	Little change	Less	Not applicable	1968–1974 (N)	1974–1980 (N)
Enrolled students (tuition and fees)	73	21	6	65	32	3		(1,163)	(1,140)
Continuing education and related services	59	38	3	69	30	1		(1,031)	(1,010)
Other (please indicate):	64	22	14	60	20	20		(42)	(46)

9. For each funding source, indicate the change in degree of flexibility over campus use of funds from:

| | 1974 compared to 1968 | | | 1980 compared to 1974 | | | | | |
	More	Little change	Less	More	Little change	Less	Not applicable	1968–1974 (N)	1974–1980 (N)
Local government	8	84	8	8	82	10		(471)	(442)
State government	12	66	22	14	58	28		(959)	(913)
Federal government	7	69	24	10	63	27		(1,043)	(994)
Endowment	12	85	3	17	80	3		(833)	(803)
Foundations & corporations	12	82	6	15	78	7		(939)	(912)
Private donors (including alumni)	18	79	3	22	74	4		(990)	(963)
Enrolled students (tuition and fees)	13	78	9	13	77	10		(1,102)	(1,059)
Continuing education and related services	17	78	5	21	73	6		(968)	(944)
Other (please indicate):	12	85	3	23	63	14		(34)	(35)

SURVEY OF PRESIDENTS' RESPONSE TO CHANGES IN ENROLLMENTS AND FINANCING (Cont'd)

	1974 compared to 1968			1980 compared to 1974			1968–1974 (N)	1974–1980 (N)
10. Indicate shift in arguments used to obtain additional funding from your primary funding source:	Extensive	Some	Very little	Extensive	Some	Very little		
Increase in enrollment	40%	27%	33%	23%	37%	40%	(1,149)	(1,122)
Serve new clientele	30	47	23	41	41	18	(1,154)	(1,131)
Reduce student/faculty ratio	9	30	61	10	34	56	(1,146)	(1,122)
Increase faculty salaries	47	42	11	45	46	9	(1,190)	(1,155)
Meet rising cost of employee benefits, energy, etc.	53	39	8	61	34	5	(1,179)	(1,150)
New academic programs	39	50	11	40	48	12	(1,186)	(1,154)
Improve quality of instruction	40	49	11	46	46	8	(1,182)	(1,159)
Expand public service activities	26	42	32	36	41	23	(1,158)	(1,134)
Expand organized research	6	25	69	9	31	60	(1,076)	(1,058)
Expand student services	22	55	23	21	57	22	(1,174)	(1,152)
Other (please indicate):	81	12	7	71	15	14	(43)	(41)

III. ACADEMIC PROGRAMS

	From 1968 to 1974			From 1974 to 1980				1968–1974 (N)	1974–1980 (N)
11. For each general academic area, indicate changes in enrollment at the undergraduate level:	Increase	Little change	Decrease	Increase	Little change	Decrease	Not applicable		
Fine arts	52%	34%	14%	36%	57%	7%		(998)	(955)
Humanities	32	42	26	21	65	14		(1,017)	(973)
Foreign languages	14	23	63	10	50	40		(1,000)	(950)

	From 1968 to 1974			From 1974 to 1980				1968–1974 (N)	1974–1980 (N)
	Increase	Little change	Decrease	Increase	Little change	Decrease	Not applicable		
Social sciences	56	31	13	38	54	8		(1,035)	(980)
Biological sciences	58	34	8	44	53	3		(1,025)	(971)
Physical sciences & mathematics ..	32	43	25	30	64	6		(1,020)	(971)
Engineering	26	38	36	46	48	6		(500)	(481)
Education	35	29	36	16	53	31		(903)	(846)
Business	73	21	6	74	25	1		(903)	(881)
Health sciences	80	19	1	75	24	1		(784)	(768)
Architecture	32	57	11	22	69	9		(241)	(231)
Agriculture	50	39	11	42	49	9		(262)	(266)
Other vocational/technical (two-year)	81	13	6	83	15	2		(477)	(475)
Other (please indicate) :	78	17	5	68	26	6		(107)	(107)

12. For each level, indicate extent of elimination or consolidation of courses for purposes of reallocating resources:

	From 1968 to 1974			From 1974 to 1980				1968–1974 (N)	1974–1980 (N)
	Extensive	Some	Very little	Extensive	Some	Very little	Not applicable		
Undergraduate	5	45	50	14	61	25		(1,110)	(1,079)
Graduate	3	29	68	7	58	35		(423)	(418)
Professional	3	27	70	4	48	48		(307)	(297)
Other (specify) :	22	45	33	18	36	46		(9)	(11)

13. For each level, indicate extent of elimination or consolidation of programs for purposes of reallocating resources:

	From 1968 to 1974			From 1974 to 1980				1968–1974 (N)	1974–1980 (N)
	Extensive	Some	Very little	Extensive	Some	Very little	Not applicable		
Undergraduate	3%	38%	59%	9%	54%	37%		(1,091)	(1,053)
Graduate	3	27	70	7	50	43		(421)	(412)
Professional	2	22	76	3	40	57		(303)	(296)
Other (specify):	10	50	40	15	46	39		(10)	(13)

14. For each level, indicate change in number of instructional programs:

	From 1968 to 1974			From 1974 to 1980				1968–1974 (N)	1974–1980 (N)
	Increase	Little change	Decrease	Increase	Little change	Decrease	Not applicable		
Undergraduate	57	38	5	34	57	9		(1,137)	(1,101)
Graduate	60	34	6	34	55	11		(426)	(430)
Professional	47	51	2	36	61	3		(316)	(314)
Extension, evening, and/or continuing education	72	24	4	83	16	1		(727)	(728)

15. For each type of "new student," indicate change in number of instructional programs designed to serve:

	From 1968 to 1974			From 1974 to 1980			1968–1974 (N)	1974–1980 (N)
	Increase	Little change	Decrease	Increase	Little change	Decrease		
Ethnic minority	49	50	1	33	65	2	(1,094)	(1,054)
Adult over 22	57	42	1	75	24	1	(1,078)	(1,046)
Evening	61	36	3	75	24	1	(999)	(977)
Off-campus	63	33	4	76	22	2	(884)	(884)

	From 1968 to 1974			From 1974 to 1980				1968–1974 (N)	1974–1980 (N)
16. Indicate changes in extent of use of various teaching-learning modes as a result of changes in enrollment and/or funds:	Increase	Little change	Decrease	Increase	Little change	Decrease	Not applicable		
Lecture sections	13%	69%	18%	15%	64%	22%		(1,183)	(1,151)
Recitation/discussion sections ...	26	70	4	22	71	7		(1,178)	(1,141)
Seminars	44	54	2	41	56	3		(1,135)	(1,107)
Laboratory work	27	70	3	29	69	2		(1,148)	(1,121)
Self-study techniques (CAI, video and audio tapes, independent study, etc.)	70	30	+	82	18	+		(1,155)	(1,138)
Field work, internships, nonresident periods	66	34	+	76	24	+		(1,093)	(1,078)
Other (please specify) :	69	26	5	63	37	+		(19)	(19)
17. Changes in faculty teaching load (contact hours)	16	68	16	25	70	5		(1,083)	(1,068)

SURVEY OF PRESIDENTS' RESPONSE TO CHANGES IN ENROLLMENTS AND FINANCING (Cont'd)

IV. FACULTY AND STAFF

18. Changes in the absolute number of faculty and staff:	1974 compared to 1968			1980 compared to 1974				1968–1974 (N)	1974–1980 (N)
	Increase over 5%	Little change	Decrease over 5%	Increase over 5%	Little change	Decrease over 5%	Not applicable		
Total instructional faculty	67%	19%	14%	37%	53%	10%		(1,164)	(1,117)
Tenured faculty	69	27	4	46	48	6		(1,021)	(992)
Nontenured faculty	50	27	23	30	49	21		(1,068)	(1,039)
Research (only) faculty	22	71	7	15	80	5		(325)	(322)
Part-time faculty	53	37	10	42	49	9		(1,182)	(1,097)
Administrators, upper level	32	62	6	11	86	3		(1,179)	(1,145)
Administrators, middle level	45	47	8	19	75	6		(1,155)	(1,125)
Clerical staff	60	33	7	31	64	5		(1,180)	(1,144)
Maintenance staff	49	40	11	31	65	4		(1,167)	(1,185)

19. Changes in the number of professional staff in the following administrative areas:

Admissions, student recruitment	59	39	2	32	67	1	(1,195) (1,142)
Public and governmental relations	33	65	2	18	81	1	(1,000) (978)
Development, fund-raising	44	52	4	36	63	1	(1,025) (1,000)
Instructional and staff development	31	66	3	29	70	1	(1,078) (1,057)
Financial management	38	60	2	19	80	1	(1,163) (1,135)
Program evaluation	23	76	1	31	69	+	(1,035) (1,026)
Institutional planning and research	37	60	3	33	67	1	(1,079) (1,063)

SURVEY OF PRESIDENTS' RESPONSE TO CHANGES IN ENROLLMENTS AND FINANCING (Cont'd)

	From 1968 to 1974			From 1974 to 1980			1968–1974 (N)	1974–1980 (N)
	Yes	No	Don't know	Prob-ably yes	Prob-ably no	Don't know		
20. For each group, indicate if collective bargaining agreements in effect at any time:								
Faculty	13%	87%	+	32%	52%	16%	(1,186)	(1,160)
Teaching assistants	4	96	+	12	71	17	(1,085)	(1,053)
Clerical staff	11	88	1	27	58	15	(1,178)	(1,150)
Maintenance staff	23	76	1	37	48	15	(1,178)	(1,141)
21. Tenure abolished?	4	95	1	8	79	13	(1,081)	(1,050)

	From 1968 to 1974			From 1974 to 1980			1968–1974 (N)	1974–1980 (N)
	Increase	Little change	Decrease	Increase	Little change	Decrease		
22. Incentives for early retirement:	13%	86%	1%	43%	56%	1%	(1,167)	(1,150)
23. Systematic efforts to evaluate faculty teaching competence:	69	31	+	82	18	+	(1,194)	(1,177)
24. Systematic efforts to retrain faculty for new or related fields or functions:	22	78	+	53	47	+	(1,180)	(1,163)
25. Rigor of standards for faculty promotions or merit increases:	49	50	1	67	32	1	(1,175)	(1,162)
26. Rigor of faculty tenure standards:	44	54	2	63	36	1	(1,082)	(1,060)

V. STUDENT SERVICES AND ADMISSIONS

	1974 compared to 1968			1980 compared to 1974			Not appli- cable	1968– 1974 (N)	1974– 1980 (N)
	Extensive	Some	Very little	Extensive	Some	Very little			
27. For each type of student, indicate emphasis on active recruitment:									
Early admissions from high school	14	54	32	34	50	16		(1,092)	(1,065)
Traditional student	65	30	5	70	27	3		(1,174)	(1,146)
Transfer student	38	43	19	56	32	12		(1,138)	(1,108)
Ethnic minority	51	41	8	52	43	5		(1,175)	(1,141)
Low-income	39	47	14	45	46	9		(1,155)	(1,123)
Adult over 22	38	39	23	66	25	9		(1,138)	(1,105)
Off-campus	35	39	26	58	29	13		(958)	(945)
Evening	41	37	22	67	24	9		(1,012)	(989)
Previous dropout	14	38	48	31	40	29		(1,056)	(1,028)
28. For each level, indicate extent of modification of admission standards to increase enrollments:									
Undergraduate	8	33	59	8	33	59		(1,106)	(1,052)
Graduate	3	15	82	4	24	72		(428)	(417)
Professional	2	13	85	2	21	77		(311)	(310)
29. For each level, indicate extent of limits set on enrollments in some fields to enable expansion in other fields:									
Undergraduate	2	17	81	4	22	74		(916)	(870)
Graduate	1	16	83	4	26	70		(390)	(374)
Professional	3	14	83	5	24	71		(270)	(264)

SURVEY OF PRESIDENTS' RESPONSE TO CHANGES IN ENROLLMENTS AND FINANCING (Cont'd)

	From 1968 to 1974			From 1974 to 1980			1968–1974 (N)	1974–1980 (N)
30. For each student service, indicate change in budgetary priority:	Increase	Little change	Decrease	Increase	Little change	Decrease		
Housing	28%	63%	9%	21%	70%	9%	(989)	(974)
Health services	34	62	4	26	69	5	(1,141)	(1,127)
Personal counseling	58	39	3	47	50	3	(1,187)	(1,169)
Vocational counseling	51	47	2	61	38	1	(1,165)	(1,160)
Academic advising	47	52	1	54	46	+	(1,186)	(1,170)
Financial aids	82	17	1	66	33	1	(1,184)	(1,172)

VI. MANAGEMENT PRACTICES

	1974 compared to 1968			1980 compared to 1974				1968–1974 (N)	1974–1980 (N)
31. Changes in use of various planning/management techniques:	Extensive	Some	Very little	Extensive	Some	Very little	Not applicable		
Management information system	26%	47%	27%	55%	38%	7%		(1,103)	(1,077)
Electronic data processing	47	39	14	58	37	5		(1,106)	(1,085)
Unit cost studies	22	52	26	55	39	6		(1,135)	(1,112)
Faculty workload studies	24	58	18	49	47	4		(1,163)	(1,132)
WICHE-NCHEMS products	13	36	51	32	46	22		(966)	(947)
Program budgeting/management by objectives	17	46	37	47	43	10		(1,101)	(1,083)
Simulation techniques	5	26	69	18	48	34		(1,002)	(982)
Analysis of institutional goals	36	51	13	63	34	3		(1,166)	(1,139)
Program evaluation	27	57	16	68	30	2		(1,164)	(1,139)
Market survey, needs analysis	13	49	38	48	43	9		(1,098)	(1,070)
Other (please specify) :	56	38	6	81	19	+		(16)	(16)

	From 1968 to 1974				From 1974 to 1980				
	Helped	No effect	Hindered		Helped	No effect	Hindered	No plan	
32. Program performance audits by outside agencies:	11	41	48	(1,048)	21	54	25		(1,015)
33. Reductions in funding departmental research in order to support some other functions:	3	22	75	(625)	4	29	67		(614)
34. Increase in credit hours per faculty contact hour:	4	29	67	(1,052)	9	41	50		(1,038)
35. Physical plant maintenance deferred:	11	43	46	(1,122)	4	47	49		(1,102)
36. Extent to which enrollment level is controlled by the legislature, coordinating agency, or some external agency:	13	21	66	(774)	16	28	56		(753)
37. Effect on your institution of the following master plans:							Hindered plan	No plan	
Institutional	86	12	2	(955)	95	4	1		(1023)
System	58	31	11	(456)	71	22	7		(499)
Statewide	47	37	16	(663)	63	20	17		(723)

SURVEY OF PRESIDENTS' RESPONSE TO CHANGES IN ENROLLMENTS AND FINANCING (Cont'd)

	From 1968 to 1974			From 1974 to 1980				1968–1974 (N)	1974–1980 (N)
	Increase	Same	Decrease	Increase	Same	Decrease	Not applicable		
38. Shifts in the locus of general decision authority:									
From department to campus administration	22%	57%	21%	22%	67%	11%		(1,065)	(996)
From campus to system board	35	56	9	31	61	8		(656)	(630)
From board to coordinating agency	33	63	4	48	48	4		(522)	(510)
From board to state budget and finance (governor)	45	52	3	47	48	5		(545)	(545)
From board to state legislature	37	59	4	45	51	4		(551)	(556)

VII.   IDENTIFICATION QUESTIONS

For each of the questions below, check the one alternative that best describes your institution. (Additional descriptive information will be obtained from the USOE Higher Education Directory, 1973-74.)

(N)

(1,212)   **39. Location**
  8% Center of (downtown in) a large metropolitan area
  22   Elsewhere in an urban or metropolitan area
  14   Suburb of a large city
  15   Medium size city (50,000-100,000)
  41   Small town or rural area

(1,196)   **40. When did your institution first enroll college students?**
  3% Before 1800
  36   1800-1899
  28   1900-1945
  12   1946-1960
   9   1961-1965
  11   1966-1970
   1   After 1970

(1,192)   **41. Selectivity:**
  8% Freshmen mostly from top 10 percent of high school
      class
  36   Mostly from the top 40 percent
  54   Essentially open admissions
   2   No freshman admissions

(1,117)   **42. Level of federal support, 1973-74:**
  5% More than $14,000,000
   5   $6,000,000 to $14,000,000
  90   Less than $6,000,000

(1,208)   **43. Total enrollment (headcount, all categories of students):**
  29% Less than 1,000
  42   1,000 to 4,999
  16   5,000 to 11,999
   8   12,000 to 20,000
   5   More than 20,000

SURVEY OF PRESIDENTS' RESPONSE TO CHANGES
IN ENROLLMENTS AND FINANCING (Cont'd)

(989)   1. What specific major changes in programs and functions do you expect to make in the next five years?

(1,003)   2. What are your chief difficulties in adjusting to the leveling of enrollment and funding?

3. Does the leveling of enrollment and funding enhance or impair the quality of:

(941)   a. students?   29%   45%   Neither   21%
         (Please   enhances   impairs   Both   1
         explain)   Don't know   4

(952)   b. faculty?   38%   44%   Neither   12%
         (Please   enhances   impairs   Both   2
         explain)   Don't know   4

(933)   c. programs?   32%   54%   Neither   9%
         (Please   enhances   impairs   Both   2
         explain)   Don't know   3

(1,126)   4. Looking ahead to the next five years, is the character of your institution likely to undergo any radical change, such as merger, consolidation, or closure?
         10% yes   83% no   7% other

(1,134)   5. Do you plan a change in the student/faculty ratio?
         35% yes   63% no   2% other
         If yes, in what areas or levels? What would be the change in the ratio?

Note: A + in the table indicates less than .5 percent.

Appendix B

Technical Notes Regarding Survey Procedures

In February 1974, the Center for Research and Development in Higher Education initiated a study of presidential perceptions of institutional responses to declining enrollment growth and fiscal stringency. Several areas of concern were delineated in discussions with staff members of the Carnegie Council on Policy Studies in Higher Education, sponsors of the project:

- Reallocation of resources among functions
- Instructional program changes
- Personnel practices
- Management practices
- Physical plant
- Success of response (to so-called steady state conditions)
- Future projections

The conceptual framework informing the data collection and analysis was, of course, refined in light of subsequent discussions, preliminary tabulations, and the like.

Pretest

By May, the project staff, with the help of an outside consultant from the Educational Testing Service, had decided on specific items for a pretest questionnaire. The pretest instrument was sent to the presidents of 48 institutions of higher education in Northern California on May 27. A cover letter describing the purposes of the survey and soliciting cooperation was signed by Clark Kerr for the Carnegie Council and Lyman Glenny for the Center. Telephone calls were made to each institution by the project staff in early June in order to elicit further comments regarding the questionnaire and responses to it.[1] Thirty-one institutions in the pretest sample responded. Their comments and criticisms guided the CRDHE staff in making the following adjustments to the pretest instrument:

1. Removal of a future time frame, "1980–1984"
2. Removal of selected qualifiers to the response category of "little change"
3. The decision to ask about "real dollars" instead of "current dollars" in the question regarding expenditures per FTE student
4. The decision to limit the inquiry regarding curriculum trends to the undergraduate level, and
5. Addition of "quality indices" in the open-ended Discussion Questions

During the two weeks from June 3 to 17, the staff considered the pretest results and telephone interview comments. Subsequently, a final version of the questionnaire was devised and printed.

The final questionnaire was intended to elicit an institutional perspective (ideally that of the president) from institutions of higher education across the country. The total mailing sample was composed of 2,497 institutions. This figure was slightly less than the number on the original Carnegie mailing list and different from the number of institutions in the Di-

[1]In most cases, the presidents had not filled out the questionnaire. Usually, the questionnaire had been routed to the Office of Institutional Research.

rectory of Institutions of Higher Education published by the U.S. Office of Education, for the following reasons:

1. Institutions offering only degrees in religion, with enrollments of less than 125, were eliminated from the sample.
2. "System" offices were also eliminated from the sample. It was felt that their responses would not really reflect an "institutional posture." However, in a few instances, the central campus office filled out a single questionnaire for several branches, which we accepted as representing one institution, if it was from a community college system office.

Questionnaire

The questionnaire was developed in light of the questions and issues identified in the Center's proposal to the Carnegie Council. The bulk of the questions dealt with two time frames: 1968–1974 and 1974–1980, with the typical option for responses being "increase," "little change," or "decrease," within each time frame. Open-ended discussion questions were included at the end of the instrument to allow for more informal and less "forced" responses. Answers to these discussion questions were transcribed verbatim and later tallied for recurring themes that might serve to illuminate findings from the standard, multiple-choice items.

Mail Out

The first mail out of the final questionnaire was on July 2. One week later, a reminder postcard was sent to all presidents. The following week, on July 16, a duplicate questionnaire was sent to those institutions which had not already returned the questionnaire.

The "cut-off" date for the receipt of the returned questionnaire was tentatively set at mid-July. By July 25, however, only 30 percent of the total sample had returned questionnaires, and it was decided to extend the cut-off date to August 16. By that time, only 39 percent of the institutions had responded. In an effort to gain a 50 percent response rate, the cut-off date was again extended, this time to mid-September.

By September 16, the desired 50 percent response rate had been achieved (presumably because many presidents had returned from summer vacation). The number of usable replies was 1,227, or approximately 50 percent of the initial sample.

Respondents

It was hoped that *presidents* of institutions would respond to the questionnaire. Based on the first 1,053 replies, however, we know that only half the questionnaires were completed by the chief executive officer. Others who completed the questionnaire are shown below:

President	483
Vice President	111
Dean	117
Director (usually of Institutional Research)	137
Others	156
Blank	59

We have supplemented the survey data with information on institutional characteristics derived from the Higher Education General Information Survey (HEGIS VI), conducted by the National Center for Educational Statistics, U.S. Office of Education. We have also used information from interviews with institutional leaders in several states, conducted within the context of the Center's Study of State Budgeting for Higher Education, a three-year project jointly funded by the National Institute of Education (NIE) and the Ford Foundation. And we have followed-up by telephone a small sample of our respondents in private two-year institutions who expressed optimism about the future despite depressing experiences in the recent past.

Appendix C

Reference Tables

Table 22. Sample universe and rate of response, by Carnegie type and control

Carnegie type and control	Sample universe	Responding institutions	
		Number	Percent of sample universe
Carnegie type			
Research I	50	32	64
Research II	35	25	71
Other doctoral I	53	36	68
Other doctoral II	28	16	57
Comprehensive I	305	176	58
Comprehensive II	133	79	59
Liberal arts I	143	93	65
Liberal arts II	529	244	46
Two-year	912	416	46
Professional	309	110	36
Control			
Public	1,178	618	52
Private	1,319	609	46
Total	2,497	1,227	49

Note: For an explanation of the categories of institutions, see Carnegie Commission on Higher Education (1973).

Table 23. Sample universe and rate of response, by selected institutional
characteristics

Institutional characteristics	Sample universe	Responding institutions	
		Number	Percent of sample universe
Affiliation			
Public	1,178	618	52
Private, independent	630	306	49
Private, affiliated	689	303	44
Current enrollment (HEGIS)			
1-199	176	51	29
200-499	312	121	39
500-999	506	228	45
1,000-2,499	642	329	51
2,500-4,999	311	172	55
5,000-9,999	261	150	57
10,000-19,999	138	96	70
20,000 and over	64	42	66
Not reported	87	38	44
Ethnic character			
Predominantly white	2,410	1,195	50
Predominantly black	87	32	37
Census region			
Northeast (Connecticut, Massachusetts, Maine, New Hampshire, Rhode Island, and Vermont)	238	120	50
Middle Atlantic (New Jersey, New York, and Pennsylvania)	388	178	46
East North Central (Illinois, Indiana, Michigan, Ohio, and Wisconsin)	387	198	51
West North Central (Iowa, Kansas, Minnesota, Missouri, Nebraska, North Dakota, and South Dakota)	287	153	53
South Atlantic (Delaware, Florida, Georgia, Maryland, North Carolina, Virginia, West Virginia, and DC)	385	193	50

Table 23. Sample universe and rate of response, by
selected institutional characteristics (Cont'd.)

		Responding institutions	
Institutional characteristics	*Sample universe*	*Number*	*Percent of sample universe*
East South Central (Alabama, Kentucky, Mississippi, and Tennessee)	192	66	34
West South Central (Arkansas, Texas, Louisiana, and Oklahoma)	200	81	40
Mountain (Arizona, Colorado, Idaho, Montana, Nevada, New Mexico, Utah, and Wyoming)	109	63	58
Pacific (Alaska, California, Hawaii, Oregon, and Washington)	305	174	57
Not reported	6	1	a
Total	2,497	1,227	49

a Not calculated; base less than 15 cases.

Table 24. Change in FTE enrollment, 1968–1974, by Carnegie type and control (in percentages of responding institutions)

Change in FTE enrollment	Public institutions, total	Private institutions		
		Total	Indepen-dent	Religious
Research & doctoral universities	(N = 68)	(N = 39)	(N = 29)	(N = 10)
Increased	72	46	52	a
Little change, decreased	28	54	48	a
Comprehensive colleges & universities	(N = 166)	(N = 80)	(N = 37)	(N = 43)
Increased	70	41	38	44
Little change	16	30	30	30
Decreased	14	29	32	26
Liberal arts colleges	(N = 19)	(N = 301)	(N = 125)	(N = 176)
Increased	79	42	46	38
Little change	16	30	30	31
Decreased	5	28	24	31
Two-year institutions	(N = 326)	(N = 70)	(N = 30)	(N = 40)
Increased	83	39	37	40
Little change, decreased	17	61	63	60
Professional schools	(N = 19)	(N = 79)	(N = 57)	(N = 22)
Increased	74	57	67	32
Little change, decreased	26	43	33	68

a Not calculated; base less than 15 cases.

Note: "Increase" and "decrease" denote changes in enrollment of more than 10 percent. "Little change" denotes a change of up to ± 10 percent.

Table 25. Percentages of institutions with selected characteristics, by change in FTE enrollment 1968–1974, Carnegie type, and control

Change in FTE enrollment	(N)	Institutional characteristics						
		Single campus (not multi-)	Highest degree: baccalaureate	Enroll women only	Teacher preparatory program	Occupational program	Professional program	Open admissions policy
Research & doctoral universities								
Public: Increased	(49)	35	a	a	98	31	100	23
Little change, decreased	(19)	47	a	a	95	58	100	37
Private: Increased	(18)	94	a	a	72	6	89	a
Little change, decreased	(21)	81	a	a	76	14	100	5
Comprehensive colleges and universities								
Public: Increased	(116)	47	11	a	100	23	58	43
Little change	(27)	82	19	4	96	44	41	52
Decreased	(24)	79	17	a	96	50	33	91
Private: Increased	(33)	94	12	6	94	3	70	18
Little change	(24)	83	25	4	92	21	83	13
Decreased	(23)	100	30	a	96	17	57	22

Liberal arts, public & private							
Increased	(141)	89	60	5	75	6	32	36
Little change	(94)	97	81	17	86	3	21	24
Decreased	(85)	98	88	24	91	4	14	39
Two-year institutions							
Public: Increased	(273)	69	a	a	a	99	2	99
Little change, decreased	(54)	83	a	a	a	100	a	98
Private: Increased	(27)	100	4	15	4	67	a	70
Little change, decreased	(43)	95	2	14	2	58	a	74
Professional schools, public & private							
Increased	(59)	83	29	1	14	12	97	29
Little change, decreased	(39)	92	39	2	26	15	95	48
Total	(1,227)	79	27	5	52	41	36	54

a No observations.

Note: "Increase" and "decrease" denote changes in enrollment of more than 10 percent. "Little change" denotes a change of up to ± 10 percent.

Table 26. Enrollment size of institutions, by change in FTE enrollment 1968–1974, Carnegie type, and control (in percentages of responding institutions)

Change in FTE enrollment	(N)	Number of students (in 1,000s)				
		Less than 1	1 to 4	5 to 11	12 to 20	Over 20
Research & doctoral universities						
Public:						
Increased	(49)	a	a	20	35	45
Little change, decreased	(19)	a	a	16	32	52
Private:						
Increased	(18)	a	22	44	17	17
Little change, decreased	(21)	a	19	48	19	14
Comprehensive colleges and universities						
Public:						
Increased	(114)	1	37	42	15	5
Little change	(26)	a	50	38	8	4
Decreased	(24)	8	59	25	8	a
Private:						
Increased	(32)	a	84	13	3	a
Little change	(24)	a	71	25	4	a
Decreased	(23)	4	87	5	4	a
Liberal arts, public & private						
Increased	(141)	35	60	4	a	1
Little change	(93)	42	57	1	a	a
Decreased	(83)	72	28	a	a	a
Two-year institutions						
Public:						
Increased	(270)	11	45	25	13	6
Little change, decreased	(53)	36	49	7	6	2
Private:						
Increased	(27)	85	11	4	a	a
Little change, decreased	(42)	86	14	a	a	a
Professional schools, public & private						
Increased	(58)	64	34	2	a	a
Little change, decreased	(37)	78	19	3	a	a

a No observations.

Note: "Increase" and "decrease" denote changes in enrollment of more than 10 percent. "Little change" denotes a change of up to ± 10 percent.

Table 27. Location of institutions by change in FTE enrollment 1968–1974, Carnegie type, and control (in percentages of responding institutions)

Change in FTE enrollment	(N)	Down-town metro area	Other urban metro area	Suburb large city	Me-dium size city	Small town, rural area
Research & doctoral universities						
Public:						
Increased	(49)	8	31	8	22	31
Little change, decreased	(19)	16	26	11	21	26
Private:						
Increased	(18)	28	33	17	11	11
Little change, decreased	(21)	14	71	a	14	a
Comprehensive colleges & universities						
Public:						
Increased	(115)	10	24	13	11	42
Little change	(27)	11	11	a	15	63
Decreased	(24)	a	4	a	8	88
Private:						
Increased	(33)	9	24	21	30	15
Little change	(24)	21	25	21	21	12
Decreased	(23)	13	22	22	17	26
Liberal arts, public & private						
Increased	(140)	4	21	18	14	43
Little change	(94)	1	17	14	17	51
Decreased	(84)	1	17	21	13	48
Two-year institutions						
Public:						
Increased	(266)	7	15	17	19	42
Little change, decreased	(53)	4	8	2	11	75
Private:						
Increased	(27)	22	15	18	15	30
Little change, decreased	(42)	17	10	14	2	57
Professional schools, public & private						
Increased	(58)	17	50	12	9	12
Little change, decreased	(39)	18	39	13	18	12

[a] No observations.

Note: "Increase" and "decrease" denote changes in enrollment of more than 10 percent. "Little change" denotes a change of up to ± 10 percent.

Table 28. Percentages of institutions in each census region, by change in FTE enrollment 1968–1974, and control

Control and change in FTE enrollment	North East	Mid Atlantic	East North	West North	South	East South	West South	Mountain	Pacific	Total
						Central				
(N)	(98)	(151)	(168)	(131)	(177)	(60)	(76)	(57)	(152)	(1,071) [a]
Public										
Increased	33	38	36	30	46	48	40	63	56	42
Little change	4	3	7	13	7	8	16	11	8	8
Decreased	[b]	1	5	11	2	2	8	9	3	4
Private										
Increased	28	24	20	15	18	13	17	7	20	19
Little change	21	17	16	14	15	15	9	3	8	14
Decreased	14	17	16	17	12	14	10	7	5	13
Total	100%	100%	100%	100%	100%	100%	100%	100%	100%	100%

[a] Professional schools excluded from analysis.

[b] No observations.

Note: "Increase" and "decrease" denote changes in enrollment of more than 10 percent. "Little change" denotes a change of up to ± 10 percent.

Table 23 shows the states included in each region.

Table 29. Change in headcount enrollment from fall 1971 to fall 1973 in institutions reporting little change or a decrease of more than 10 percent in FTE enrollment 1968–1974, by Carnegie type and control (in percentages of responding institutions)

| | | Change in headcount 1971–1973 | | | | | |
| | | Increased | | Decreased | | | |
Change in FTE enrollment, 1968–1974	(N)	Over 5%	1%–5%	1%–5%	6%–10%	11%–15%	Over 15%
Research & doctoral universities							
Public:							
Little change, decreased	(19)	a	32	32	16	5	5
Private:							
Little change, decreased	(21)	14	14	38	14	5	10
Comprehensive colleges & universities							
Public:							
Little change	(27)	19	19	26	15	15	3
Decreased	(24)	a	a	12	25	17	29
Private:							
Little change	(24)	13	25	21	25	8	a
Decreased	(23)	a	4	13	26	17	30
Liberal arts, public & private							
Little change	(94)	24	25	25	6	3	10
Decreased	(85)	4	5	11	20	14	34
Two-year institutions							
Public:							
Little change, decreased	(54)	23	12	7	26	11	12
Private:							
Little change, decreased	(43)	18	12	7	14	9	21
Professional schools, public & private							
Little change, decreased	(39)	8	13	15	10	13	16
All institutions with increased FTE enrollment, 1968–1974	(716)	64	17	5	2	1	1

ᵃ No observations.

Note: "Increase" and "decrease" denote changes in enrollment of more than 10 percent. "Little change" denotes a change of up to ± 10 percent.

Table 30. Comparison of enrollment projections made in the late 1960s to actual 1974 enrollment, by type of institution and control (in percentages of responding institutions)

Type of institution and control	(N)	*1974 enrollment compared to projected enrollment*		
		Equalled or exceeded projection	*Fell short by 1–14 percent*	*Fell short by 15 percent or more*
Universities				
Public	(136)	35	47	18
Independent	(53)	62	32	6
Religious	(23)	56	35	9
Colleges (four-five year)				
Public	(119)	43	40	17
Independent	(171)	49	34	17
Religious	(194)	28	48	24
Two-year institutions				
Public	(306)	60	31	9
Independent	(36)	36	25	39
Religious	(32)	22	53	25
Total	(1,074)	46	38	16

Note: "Universities" include institutions offering a predoctorate or doctorate degree beyond the master's as the highest level of training. "Colleges" include institutions that offer a baccalaureate, a first-professional, or a master's degree as the highest level of training. "Two-year institutions" offer no more than an associate degree.

Table 31. Comparison of enrollment projections made in the late 1960s to actual 1974 enrollment, by change in FTE enrollment 1968–1974, Carnegie type, and control (in percentages of responding institutions)

Change in FTE enrollment	(N)	*1974 enrollment compared to projected enrollment*		
		Equalled or exceeded projection	*Fell short by 1–14 percent*	*Fell short by 15 percent or more*
Research & doctoral universities				
Public:				
Increased	(46)	54	41	4
Little change, decreased	(18)	6	39	55
Private:				
Increased	(14)	64	36	a
Little change, decreased	(17)	41	41	18
Comprehensive colleges & universities				
Public:				
Increased	(108)	44	43	13
Little change	(25)	20	64	16
Decreased	(23)	4	57	39
Private:				
Increased	(30)	80	20	a
Little change	(21)	19	71	10
Decreased	(20)	5	45	50
Liberal arts, public & private				
Increased	(118)	57	35	8
Little change	(83)	36	52	12
Decreased	(69)	a	41	59
Two-year institutions				
Public:				
Increased	(248)	66	27	7
Little change, decreased	(52)	29	52	19
Private:				
Increased	(23)	61	26	13
Little change, decreased	(37)	11	49	40

Cont'd.

Table 31. Comparison of enrollment projections made in the late 1960s to actual 1974 enrollment, by change in FTE enrollment 1968–1974, Carnegie type, and control (in percentages of responding institutions) (Cont'd.)

		1974 enrollment compared to projected enrollment		
Change in FTE enrollment	*(N)*	*Equalled or exceeded projection*	*Fell short by 1–14 percent*	*Fell short by 15 percent or more*
Professional schools, public & private				
Increased	(49)	80	16	4
Little change, decreased	(28)	29	57	14

[a]No observations.

Note: "Increase" and "decrease" denote changes in enrollment of more than 10 percent. "Little change" denotes a change of up to ± 10 percent.

Table 32. Percentages of institutions with selected characteristics, by change in real operating expenditures per FTE student 1968–1974, Carnegie type, and control

Change in expenditures per FTE student	(N)	Single campus (not multi-)	Highest degree: bacca-laureate	Enroll women only	Teacher prepara-tory prog.	Occupa-tional program	Profes-sional program	Open admis-sions policy
				Institutional characteristics				
Research & doctoral universities								
Public:								
Increased	(22)	55	a	a	96	41	100	32
Little change, decreased	(41)	32	a	a	98	42	100	22
Private:								
Increased	(16)	87	a	a	63	6	100	6
Little change, decreased	(19)	95	a	a	84	16	95	a
Comprehensive colleges & universities								
Public:								
Increased	(74)	60	15	a	99	28	47	50
Little change, decreased	(79)	58	13	1	99	32	56	51

Private:							
Increased	(45)	91	22	2	91	16	69	13
Little change, decreased	(26)	96	27	4	96	12	73	15
Liberal arts, public & private							
Increased	(160)	96	81	17	84	7	25	35
Little change, decreased	(121)	93	68	8	79	1	22	28
Two-year institutions							
Public:							
Increased	(157)	73	a	a	a	99	2	99
Little change, decreased	(140)	67	a	a	a	99	1	98
Private:							
Increased	(44)	100	a	9	a	50	a	75
Little change, decreased	(23)	100	a	13	4	74	a	70
Professional schools, public & private							
Increased	(60)	92	33	3	22	15	95	36
Little change, decreased	(28)	89	32	a	4	11	100	38

a No observations.

Note: "Increase" and "decrease" denote changes in expenditures of more than 10 percent. "Little change" denotes a change of up to ± 10 percent.

Table 33. Change in real operating expenditures per FTE student, by change in FTE enrollment, Carnegie type, and control, 1968–1974 (in percentages of responding institutions)

| | | Change in operating expenditures | | |
| | | Increased more than | Little | Decreased more than |
Change in FTE enrollment	(N)	10 percent	change	10 percent
Research & doctoral universities				
Public:				
Increased	(46)	33	52	15
Little change, decreased	(16)	44	31	25
Private:				
Increased	(16)	38	50	12
Little change, decreased	(18)	50	33	17
Comprehensive colleges & univ.				
Public:				
Increased	(103)	53	42	5
Little change	(26)	42	54	4
Decreased	(19)	26	63	11
Private:				
Increased	(28)	64	36	a
Little change	(22)	64	36	a
Decreased	(20)	60	40	a
Liberal arts, public & private				
Increased	(119)	53	41	6
Little change	(80)	54	46	a
Decreased	(71)	68	25	7
Two-year institutions				
Public:				
Increased	(243)	55	39	6
Little change, decreased	(47)	45	51	4
Private:				
Increased	(21)	81	19	a
Little change, decreased	(41)	56	39	5
Professional schools, public & private				
Increased	(51)	73	25	2
Little change, decreased	(31)	55	35	10
Total	(1,055)	55	39	6

a No observations.

Note: "Increase" and "decrease" denote changes in enrollment of more than 10 percent. "Little change" denotes a change of up to ± 10 percent.

Table 34. Anticipated change in expenditures per FTE student, 1974–1980, by actual change 1968–1974, Carnegie type, and control (in percentages of responding institutions)

Change in expenditures per FTE student 1968–1974	*Expenditures per FTE student, 1974–1980*			
	(N)	*Increase*	*Little change*	*Decrease*
Research & doctoral universities				
Public:				
Increased	(20)	60	40	a
Little change, decreased	(38)	3	87	10
Private:				
Increased	(16)	56	44	a
Little change, decreased	(18)	6	89	5
Comprehensive colleges & universities				
Public:				
Increased	(68)	65	34	1
Little change, decreased	(77)	10	86	4
Private:				
Increased	(44)	89	11	a
Little change, decreased	(23)	13	87	a
Liberal arts, public & private				
Increased	(153)	63	34	3
Little change, decreased	(113)	19	75	6
Two-year institutions				
Public:				
Increased	(149)	81	19	a
Little change, decreased	(132)	24	69	7
Private:				
Increased	(42)	81	12	7
Little change, decreased	(20)	30	65	5
Professional schools, public & private				
Increased	(53)	77	23	a
Little change, decreased	(28)	21	71	7
Total	(1,003)	48	49	3

a No observations.

Note: "Increase" and "decrease" denote changes in expenditures of more than 10 percent. "Little change" denotes a change of up to ± 10 percent.

Table 35. Availability of capital outlay funds, by Carnegie type and control, 1968, 1974, and 1980 (in percentages of responding institutions)

Carnegie type and control	(N)	Substantial building program			Moderate building program			Primarily rehabilitation		
		1968	1974	1980	1968	1974	1980	1968	1974	1980
All institutions	(1,122, 1,145, 1,114)	53	18	10	31	43	39	16	39	51
Public										
Research universities	(34)	68	27	6	29	44	47	3	29	47
Other doctoral	(33)[a]	76	9	6	18	64	25	6	27	69
Comprehensive	(163)[a]	60	19	6	33	49	32	8	31	62
Liberal arts	(19)	53	37	5	16	32	32	32	31	63
Two-year	(302)[b]	61	26	15	25	51	42	13	22	42
Professional	(18)[b]	27	44	11	20	22	56	53	33	33
Private										
Research universities	(20)[a]	60	15	5	25	35	42	15	50	53
Other doctoral	(18)	61	17	5	33	33	39	6	50	56
Comprehensive	(80)[a]	50	9	3	34	40	33	16	51	64
Liberal arts	(292)[b]	44	12	8	37	35	42	19	53	50
Two-year	(70)[b]	32	7	10	42	29	43	26	64	47
Professional	(80)[a]	48	21	14	24	39	34	29	39	52

[a]Ns vary by 1 or 2 for one or two of the three years.

[b]Ns vary from 3 to 8 for one or two of the three years.

Table 36. Availability of capital outlay funds, by institutional type and control, 1968, 1974, and 1980 (in percentages of responding institutions)

Institutional type and control	(N)	Substantial building program			Moderate building program			Primarily rehabilitation		
		1968	1974	1980	1968	1974	1980	1968	1974	1980
Universities										
Public	(139)	68	19	6	28	55	36	4	27	58
Independent	(61)	62	15	7	26	37	36	12	46	57
Religious	(27)	48	22	8	33	41	46	19	37	46
Colleges (four-five year)										
Public	(125)	52	26	7	29	38	33	19	35	60
Independent	(183)	46	13	11	33	33	38	20	54	51
Religious	(224)	43	12	7	37	39	39	20	49	54
Two-year institutions										
Public	(309)	61	26	15	25	51	42	13	22	42
Independent	(36)	35	8	15	33	22	50	32	69	35
Religious	(37)	28	5	6	46	33	36	26	62	58
Total	(1,145)	53	18	10	31	43	39	16	39	51

Note: "Universities" include institutions offering a predoctorate or doctorate degree beyond the master's as the highest level of training. "Colleges" include institutions which offer a baccalaureate, a first-professional, or a master's degree as the highest level of training. "Two-year institutions" offer no more than an associate degree.

Table 37. Percentages of institutions with selected characteristics, by change in availability of capital outlay funds from 1968 to 1974, Carnegie type, and control

Change in availability of capital outlay funds from 1968 to 1974	(N)	*Institutional characteristics*			
		Admit mostly top 10 percent from high school	*Federal support $6 million or more*	*Large size*[a]	*Campus in metro-politan area or suburb*
Public universities & comprehensives					
Substantial building 1974	(45)	11	36	65	59
Moderate 1974 from substantial	(80)	2	22	78	38
Rehabilitation only 1974					
from substantial	(41)	7	23	73	27
Steady or decrease 1974	(64)	2	19	49	31
Private universities & comprehensives					
Substantial building 1974	(16)	31	19	31	57
Moderate 1974 from substantial	(32)	32	26	39	62
Rehabilitation only 1974					
from substantial	(25)	28	26	46	72
Steady or decrease 1974	(45)	13	24	38	75
Private liberal arts					
Substantial building 1974	(46)	15	2	70	47
Moderate 1974 from substantial	(50)	16	b	56	26
Rehabilitation only 1974					
from substantial	(58)	14	2	41	41
Steady or decrease 1974	(131)	10	2	49	37
Public two-year					
Substantial building 1974	(86)	b	2	50	45
Moderate 1974 from substantial	(93)	b	1	33	33
Rehabilitation only 1974					
from substantial	(31)	b	b	32	33
Steady or decrease 1974	(75)	b	3	31	20

[a]"Large size" is 5,000 or more students, except in the private liberal arts colleges where "large size" means 1,000 or more students.

[b]No observations.

Note: "Substantial building" includes institutions with substantial building in both 1968 and 1974; a shift to substantial building, 1974, from moderate building or rehabilitation only in 1968; or a shift to moderate building, 1974, from rehabilitation only in 1968.

"Steady or decrease" includes institutions with moderate building in both 1968 and 1974; rehabilitation only in 1968 and 1974; or a shift from moderate building in 1968 to rehabilitation only in 1974.

Table 38. Availability of capital outlay funds, 1974, by change in FTE enrollment 1968–1974, Carnegie type, and control (in percentages of responding institutions)

		1974		
Change in FTE enrollment, 1968–1974	*(N)*	*Substantial building program*	*Moderate building program*	*Primarily rehabilitation*
Research & doctoral universities				
Public:				
Increased	(48)	21	54	25
Little change, decreased	(18)	11	56	33
Private:				
Increased	(17)	18	29	53
Little change, decreased	(20)	15	35	50
Comprehensive colleges & universities				
Public:				
Increased	(109)	23	51	26
Little change	(26)	16	46	38
Decreased	(23)	a	48	52
Private:				
Increased	(32)	9	46	45
Little change	(24)	12	42	46
Decreased	(22)	4	28	68
Liberal arts, public & private				
Increased	(132)	18	44	38
Little change	(92)	14	33	53
Decreased	(75)	7	19	74
Two-year institutions				
Public:				
Increased	(251)	28	53	19
Little change, decreased	(50)	12	42	46
Private:				
Increased	(23)	14	43	43
Little change, decreased	(43)	2	22	76
Professional schools, public & private				
Increased	(55)	25	37	28
Little change, decreased	(35)	21	33	46

a No observations.

Note: "Increase" and "decrease" denote changes in enrollment of more than 10 percent. "Little change" denotes a change of up to ± 10 percent.

Table 39. Deferral of physical plant maintenance, by selected types of institutions and change in FTE enrollment, 1968–1974 (in percentages of responding institutions)

Change in FTE enrollment by selected types of institutions, 1968–1974	(N)	Extent to which physical plant maintenance has been deferred, 1968–1974		
		Extensive	Some	Very little
Public research & doctoral universities				
Increased	(48)	12	48	40
Little change, decreased	(16)	6	88	6
Public & private liberal arts				
Increased	(127)	54	45	1
Little change	(83)	2	48	50
Decreased	(77)	5	59	36

Note: "Increase" and "decrease" denote changes in enrollment of more than 10 percent. "Little change" denotes a change of up to ± 10 percent.

Table 40. Change in undergraduate enrollment in selected academic areas, by change in FTE enrollment, Carnegie type, and control, 1968–1974 (in percentages of responding institutions)

Change in FTE enrollment	Humanities			Physical sciences			Biological sciences		
	(N)	Increased	Decreased	(N)	Increased	Decreased	(N)	Increased	Decreased
Research & doctoral universities									
Public:									
Increased	(48)	46	15	(48)	48	15	(48)	88	2
Little change, decreased	(18)	11	56	(18)	28	22	(18)	61	6
Private:									
Increased	(16)	44	31	(16)	31	31	(16)	88	b
Little change, decreased	(18)	17	50	(19)	5	42	(19)	68	16
Comprehensive colleges & universities									
Public:									
Increased	(109)	51	20	(110)	40	16	(111)	72	2
Little change	(26)	8	46	(26)	23	15	(26)	27	19
Decreased	(22)	b	73	(24)	8	54	(24)	25	21
Private:									
Increased	(31)	42	23	(31)	23	19	(31)	71	b
Little change	(24)	8	50	(22)	14	50	(23)	52	9
Decreased	(22)	9	50	(23)	13	48	(22)	41	14

Liberal arts, public & private									
Increased	(128)	38	12	(128)	37	23	(128)	66	6
Little change	(91)	14	28	(90)	20	34	(92)	52	9
Decreased	(78)	14	47	(76)	13	45	(77)	36	23
Two-year institutions									
Public:									
Increased	(226)	48	13	(233)	51	10	(234)	68	5
Little change, decreased	(50)	18	26	(50)	22	32	(50)	34	12
Private:									
Increased	(20)	10	35	(21)	10	24	(21)	38	14
Little change, decreased	(32)	16	31	(31)	16	39	(31)	19	19
Professional schools, public & private									
Increased	(12)	a	a	(8)	a	a	(12)	a	a
Little change, decreased	(11)	a	a	(14)	a	a	(10)	a	a

Cont'd.

Table 40. Change in undergraduate enrollments in selected academic areas, by change in FTE enrollment, Carnegie type, and control, 1968–1974 (in percentages of responding institutions) (Cont'd.)

Change in FTE enrollment	Business			Health sciences		
	(N)	Increased	Decreased	(N)	Increased	Decreased
Research & doctoral universities						
Public:						
Increased	(44)	84	b	(43)	88	b
Little change, decreased	(17)	59	12	(15)	100	b
Private:						
Increased	(10)	a	a	(10)	a	a
Little change, decreased	(14)	a	a	(11)	a	a
Comprehensive colleges & universities						
Public:						
Increased	(99)	88	b	(86)	87	b
Little change	(22)	77	5	(23)	65	4
Decreased	(24)	67	8	(20)	90	b
Private:						
Increased	(29)	86	3	(23)	83	b
Little change	(19)	53	16	(17)	82	b
Decreased	(21)	57	24	(14)	a	a

Liberal arts, public & private						
Increased	(97)	77	4	(61)	79	2
Little change	(62)	71	10	(53)	70	2
Decreased	(64)	59	8	(49)	59	4
Two-year institutions						
Public:						
Increased	(243)	82	2	(234)	86	1
Little change, decreased	(50)	48	10	(46)	67	4
Private:						
Increased	(18)	78	17	(17)	77	6
Little change, decreased	(28)	32	25	(20)	60	b
Professional schools, public & private						
Increased	(5)	a	a	(14)	a	a
Little change, decreased	(8)	a	a	(2)	a	a

a Not calculated; base less than 15 cases.

b No observations.

Note: "Increase" and "decrease" denote changes in FTE enrollment of more than 10 percent. "Little change" denotes a change of up to ± 10 percent. Extent of "increase" and "decrease" in academic area enrollment was not specified.

Table 41. Changes in undergraduate enrollment in academic areas, actual 1968–1974 and anticipated 1974–1980, by Carnegie type and control (in percentages of responding institutions)

Fine arts / Humanities

Carnegie type and control	Fine arts 1968–1974			Fine arts 1974–1980			Humanities 1968–1974			Humanities 1974–1980		
	(N)	In-creased	De-creased	(N)	In-crease	De-crease	(N)	In-creased	De-creased	(N)	In-crease	De-crease
Public												
Research universities	(32)	66	6	(31)	38	10	(34)	44	18	(33)	24	27
Other doctoral	(33)	64	6	(31)	58	a	(33)	27	36	(31)	16	13
Comprehensive	(162)	56	12	(158)	38	6	(162)	38	31	(159)	22	15
Liberal arts	(18)	61	11	(16)	44	6	(18)	44	17	(17)	41	12
Two-year	(282)	51	12	(273)	30	10	(281)	43	16	(272)	22	15
Private												
Research universities	(16)	50	19	(15)	13	a	(19)	32	37	(18)	6	22
Other doctoral	(15)	67	13	(15)	33	7	(16)	25	44	(16)	6	13
Comprehensive	(76)	49	17	(69)	32	12	(79)	22	39	(73)	16	22
Liberal arts	(284)	51	14	(268)	39	5	(293)	23	28	(275)	20	10
Two-year	(59)	37	25	(57)	39	7	(58)	16	35	(57)	19	11
Professional	(16)	63	13	(16)	19	19	(17)	41	12	(15)	20	13

Foreign languages / Social sciences

Carnegie type and control	Foreign languages 1968–1974			Foreign languages 1974–1980			Social sciences 1968–1974			Social sciences 1974–1980		
	(N)	In-creased	De-creased	(N)	In-crease	De-crease	(N)	In-creased	De-creased	(N)	In-crease	De-crease
Public												
Research universities	(34)	35	50	(33)	18	36	(34)	77	9	(32)	47	3
Other doctoral	(33)	21	67	(31)	7	48	(33)	52	9	(31)	32	3
Comprehensive	(159)	23	48	(157)	9	40	(166)	62	18	(160)	40	9
Liberal arts	(16)	25	50	(15)	27	20	(18)	83	6	(17)	71	6
Two-year	(276)	19	55	(265)	11	47	(288)	48	14	(279)	29	12

Biological sciences | Physical sciences & mathematics

	Biological sciences						Physical sciences & mathematics					
	(N)			(N)			(N)			(N)		
Private												
Research universities	(20)	10	60	(19)	5	26	(20)	55	15	(19)	26	a
Other doctoral	(15)	27	53	(15)	13	20	(17)	47	18	(17)	41	12
Comprehensive	(79)	5	76	(74)	4	45	(80)	51	10	(75)	23	5
Liberal arts	(292)	7	75	(270)	9	37	(296)	63	10	(271)	47	6
Two-year	(55)	2	75	(52)	4	33	(60)	38	17	(58)	36	7
Professional	(15)	20	47	(12)	b	b	(17)	53	12	(15)	60	20
Public												
Research universities	(34)	85	a	(33)	76	a	(34)	44	24	(33)	36	3
Other doctoral	(33)	76	6	(31)	52	3	(33)	42	9	(31)	23	a
Comprehensive	(166)	57	7	(162)	44	2	(165)	33	21	(161)	30	7
Liberal arts	(19)	58	5	(17)	65	a	(18)	44	17	(17)	71	6
Two-year	(289)	62	6	(277)	45	3	(288)	46	14	(277)	35	4

Engineering | Health sciences

	Engineering						Health sciences					
	(N)			(N)			(N)			(N)		
Private												
Research universities	(20)	85	a	(18)	39	a	(20)	15	35	(19)	26	5
Other doctoral	(16)	69	19	(16)	25	6	(16)	19	38	(16)	13	13
Comprehensive	(78)	58	6	(72)	42	6	(78)	19	36	(74)	31	4
Liberal arts	(292)	54	12	(271)	40	3	(290)	25	33	(268)	27	8
Two-year	(56)	27	18	(54)	32	7	(56)	14	32	(54)	17	9
Professional	(16)	38	13	(13)	b	b	(14)	b	b	(12)	b	b
Public												
Research universities	(30)	23	53	(29)	76	a	(29)	97	a	(28)	96	a
Other doctoral	(23)	35	48	(21)	71	a	(30)	87	a	(28)	89	a
Comprehensive	(55)	38	20	(56)	57	2	(134)	84	1	(134)	84	a
Two-year	(240)	28	29	(234)	36	8	(285)	83	1	(274)	76	2

Cont'd.

Table 41. Changes in undergraduate enrollment in academic areas, actual 1968–1974 and anticipated 1974–1980, by Carnegie type and control (in percentages of responding institutions) (Cont'd.)

Engineering / Health sciences

Carnegie type and control	Engineering 1968–1974 (N)	In-creased	De-creased	Engineering 1974–1980 (N)	In-crease	De-crease	Health sciences 1968–1974 (N)	In-creased	De-creased	Health sciences 1974–1980 (N)	In-crease	De-crease
Private												
Research universities	(18)	22	56	(15)	60	a	(13)	b	b	(12)	b	b
Comprehensive	(32)	13	69	(29)	59	3	(54)	78	a	(53)	70	a
Liberal arts	(53)	15	34	(53)	34	8	(162)	68	2	(164)	67	1
Two-year	(19)	21	42	(16)	25	19	(39)	67	3	(37)	68	3

Business / Education

Carnegie type and control	Business 1968–1974 (N)	In-creased	De-creased	Business 1974–1980 (N)	In-crease	De-crease	Education 1968–1974 (N)	In-creased	De-creased	Education 1974–1980 (N)	In-crease	De-crease
Public												
Research universities	(33)	79	a	(32)	88	a	(32)	44	41	(31)	16	39
Other doctoral	(29)	76	7	(28)	68	a	(32)	56	25	(30)	17	50
Comprehensive	(149)	83	2	(147)	81	a	(165)	35	38	(159)	16	37
Liberal arts	(13)	b	b	(15)	100	a	(18)	56	22	(16)	25	19
Two-year	(298)	77	3	(288)	69	1	(221)	29	35	(210)	15	30
Private												
Comprehensive	(71)	69	13	(66)	68	a	(77)	29	46	(68)	10	25
Liberal arts	(220)	69	6	(215)	77	2	(276)	36	34	(257)	18	26
Two-year	(52)	52	19	(52)	65	2	(40)	33	45	(37)	11	35
Professional	(10)	b	b	(10)	b	b	(17)	65	18	(12)	b	b

Table (rotated 90° on page). Row labels at left; under each field two percentage figures are reported followed by the base number (N). Cells shown as "value / value (N)".

Top panel

	Agriculture		Architecture	
Public				
Research universities	83 / 6 (18)	61 / a (18)	78 / a (23)	41 / a (22)
Comprehensive	58 / 13 (31)	41 / 12 (32)	b / b (12)	b / b (12)
Two-year	50 / 13 (163)	42 / 10 (167)	22 / 15 (149)	13 / 13 (143)
Private				
Liberal arts	16 / 5 (19)	30 / 5 (20)	7 / 7 (15)	20 / 7 (15)

Bottom panel

	Other voc./technical (two-year)		Other	
Public				
Other doctoral	73 / a (15)	80 / a (15)	b / b (6)	b / b (5)
Comprehensive	75 / 11 (57)	80 / 2 (64)	72 / a (18)	81 / a (16)
Two-year	91 / 1 (291)	89 / 1 (281)	82 / a (17)	74 / a (19)
Private				
Comprehensive	50 / 25 (16)	b / b (14)	b / b (8)	b / b (7)
Liberal arts	69 / 10 (39)	80 / 2 (40)	83 / 4 (24)	56 / 8 (25)
Two-year	51 / 22 (37)	74 / 5 (39)	b / b (7)	b / b (9)
Professional	b / b (6)	b / b (7)	b / b (14)	b / b (15)

[a] No observations.

[b] Not calculated; base less than 15 cases.

Note: Not shown in table are certain types of institutions by Carnegie classification in which less than 15 institutions responded.

Table 42. Percentage of institutions reporting increased enrollments in more than half of their vocational programs for 1968–1974, by Carnegie type and control

Carnegie type and control	(N)[a]	Percentage of institutions	Rank order by sector
Public			
Research universities	(34)	74	2
Other doctoral	(33)	81	1
Comprehensive	(166)	60	4
Liberal arts	(18)	67	3
Two-year	(319)	58	5
Professional	(14)	57	6
Private			
Research universities	(19)	16	6
Other doctoral	(15)	40	3
Comprehensive	(81)	40	4
Liberal arts	(293)	44	2
Two-year	(64)	29	5
Professional	(41)	59	1

[a]Includes 119 institutions with only one vocational program.

Table 43. Extent of elimination or consolidation of courses for purposes of reallocating resources, actual 1968–1974 and anticipated 1974–1980, by change in FTE enrollment 1968–1974, Carnegie type, and control (in percentages of responding institutions)

Change in FTE enrollment, 1968–1974	Course elimination or consolidation					
	1968–1974			*1974–1980*		
	(N)	*Extensive*	*Very little*	*(N)*	*Extensive*	*Very little*
Research & doctoral universities						
Public:						
Increased	(47)	a	62	(47)	9	30
Little change, decreased	(19)	a	47	(19)	5	16
Private:						
Increased	(17)	a	41	(17)	18	18
Little change, decreased	(20)	10	30	(19)	5	21
Comprehensive colleges & universities						
Public:						
Increased	(109)	3	63	(109)	9	21
Little change	(27)	a	52	(27)	15	22
Decreased	(23)	9	44	(22)	27	9
Private:						
Increased	(33)	9	42	(33)	15	15
Little change	(24)	4	46	(24)	29	13
Decreased	(23)	9	48	(23)	13	22
Liberal arts, public & private						
Increased	(133)	8	52	(125)	14	27
Little change	(91)	6	44	(87)	18	20
Decreased	(84)	16	26	(80)	29	18
Two-year institutions						
Public:						
Increased	(244)	3	52	(238)	14	26
Little change, decreased	(51)	6	43	(47)	11	17
Private:						
Increased	(25)	4	44	(25)	16	32
Little change, decreased	(42)	a	52	(39)	10	28
Professional schools, public & private						
Increased	(29)	7	79	(29)	3	62
Little change, decreased	(28)	4	61	(26)	8	42

[a]No observations.

Note: "Increase" and "decrease" denote changes in enrollment of more than 10 percent. "Little change" denotes a change of up to ±10 percent.

Table 44. Change in number of professional staff in various administrative areas, actual 1968–1974 and anticipated 1974–1980, by Carnegie type and control (in percentages of responding institutions)

Administrative area	1968–1974			1974–1980		
	(N)	In-creased	Little change	(N)	In-crease	Little change
Public						
Research universities						
Admissions	(36)	56	44	(36)	25	72
Public/govt. relations	(35)	34	66	(35)	20	77
Development/fund raising	(35)	40	57	(35)	37	63
Instructional/staff devel.	(35)	43	57	(34)	32	62
Financial management	(36)	56	44	(36)	25	75
Program evaluation	(36)	42	58	(36)	44	56
Institutional plans/res.	(35)	63	34	(36)	39	61
Other doctoral universities						
Admissions	(33)	61	39	(33)	21	79
Public/govt. relations	(32)	41	56	(32)	22	78
Development/fund raising	(31)	58	39	(31)	19	81
Instructional/staff devel.	(32)	44	56	(32)	22	75
Financial management	(33)	52	46	(33)	24	73
Program evaluation	(32)	31	69	(32)	50	50
Institutional plans/res.	(32)	56	38	(32)	34	66
Comprehensive colleges & universities						
Admissions	(170)	61	38	(167)	32	66
Public/govt. relations	(159)	36	62	(155)	19	80
Development/fund raising	(148)	43	55	(144)	40	61
Instructional/staff devel.	(154)	31	66	(155)	36	62
Financial management	(169)	50	49	(165)	25	75
Program evaluation	(152)	20	79	(152)	39	61
Institutional plans/res.	(165)	47	51	(163)	37	63
Liberal arts colleges						
Admissions	(19)	79	16	(19)	74	26
Public/govt. relations	(17)	29	65	(17)	12	88
Development/fund raising	(14)	a	a	(16)	44	50
Instructional/staff devel.	(17)	47	47	(17)	41	59
Financial management	(19)	68	26	(19)	21	79
Program evaluation	(17)	41	59	(17)	53	47
Institutional plans/res.	(19)	42	53	(19)	47	53
Two-year institutions						
Admissions	(330)	57	47	(317)	34	65
Public/govt. relations	(269)	33	66	(266)	20	80
Development/fund raising	(218)	27	72	(217)	26	73

Table **44.** Change in number of professional staff in various administrative areas, actual 1968–1974 and anticipated 1974–1980, by Carnegie type and control (in percentages of responding institutions) (Cont'd)

		1968–1974			1974–1980	
Administrative area	*(N)*	*In-creased*	*Little change*	*(N)*	*In-crease*	*Little change*
Two-year institutions (Cont'd)						
Instructional/staff devel.	(315)	39	59	(308)	35	64
Financial management	(320)	40	59	(317)	21	79
Program evaluation	(302)	26	73	(299)	33	66
Institutional plans/res.	(302)	37	61	(298)	33	66
Professional schools						
Admissions	(17)	59	41	(17)	35	65
Public/govt. relations	(15)	40	60	(15)	33	60
Development/fund raising	(13)	a	a	(13)	a	a
Instructional/staff devel.	(15)	33	60	(15)	53	47
Financial management	(16)	44	56	(16)	31	69
Program evaluation	(14)	a	a	(15)	40	60
Institutional plans/res.	(15)	33	67	(16)	44	56
Private						
Research universities						
Admissions	(21)	52	43	(19)	5	95
Public/govt. relations	(21)	71	19	(19)	16	84
Development/fund raising	(21)	67	24	(19)	26	68
Instructional/staff devel.	(19)	26	68	(18)	17	83
Financial management	(21)	48	48	(19)	5	95
Program evaluation	(19)	21	74	(18)	6	94
Institutional plans/res.	(21)	33	67	(19)	16	84
Other doctoral universities						
Admissions	(19)	68	32	(18)	50	50
Public/govt. relations	(18)	50	44	(17)	18	76
Development/fund raising	(19)	42	42	(18)	44	56
Instructional/staff devel.	(15)	13	80	(15)	20	80
Financial management	(18)	56	39	(17)	12	88
Program evaluation	(15)	20	80	(15)	20	80
Institutional plans/res.	(19)	58	37	(18)	39	61
Comprehensive colleges & universities						
Admissions	(80)	73	26	(76)	29	71
Public/govt. relations	(72)	22	75	(71)	10	87
Development/fund raising	(81)	49	47	(80)	38	61
Instructional/staff devel.	(72)	24	74	(72)	15	83

Cont'd.

Table 44. Change in number of professional staff in various administrative areas, actual 1968–1974 and anticipated 1974–1980, by Carnegie type and control (in percentages of responding institutions) (Cont'd.)

Administrative area	(N)	1968–1974 In- creased	Little change	(N)	1974–1980 In- crease	Little change
Comprehensive colleges & universities (Cont'd.)						
Financial management	(81)	33	63	(80)	6	93
Program evaluation	(67)	12	87	(68)	15	85
Institutional plans/res.	(73)	30	63	(72)	24	76
Liberal arts colleges						
Admissions	(309)	67	31	(288)	30	69
Public/govt. relations	(250)	28	68	(240)	16	83
Development/fund raising	(299)	50	44	(283)	40	59
Instructional/staff devel.	(268)	23	74	(256)	23	76
Financial management	(303)	29	67	(288)	16	83
Program evaluation	(249)	18	81	(242)	25	74
Institutional plans/res.	(270)	33	64	(262)	31	68
Two-year institutions						
Admissions	(76)	59	38	(71)	35	65
Public/govt. relations	(54)	37	61	(51)	18	80
Development/fund raising	(67)	54	42	(66)	52	49
Instructional/staff devel.	(64)	25	72	(62)	31	68
Financial management	(65)	28	69	(64)	25	73
Program evaluation	(57)	25	75	(58)	33	66
Institutional plans/res.	(58)	29	71	(58)	36	64
Professional schools						
Admissions	(85)	46	52	(81)	28	70
Public/govt. relations	(58)	24	72	(60)	18	82
Development/fund raising	(79)	51	47	(78)	40	58
Instructional/staff devel.	(72)	29	71	(73)	19	81
Financial management	(82)	28	70	(81)	16	84
Program evaluation	(75)	21	77	(74)	20	78
Institutional plans/res.	(70)	21	77	(70)	26	73

[a] Not calculated; base less than 15 cases.

Note: "Increase" denotes a change of more than 5 percent. "Little change" denotes a change of up to ± 5 percent.

Table 45. Change in number of faculty, actual 1968–1974 and anticipated 1974–1980, by Carnegie type and control (by percentages of responding institutions)

| Type of faculty | (N) | 1968–1974 | | (N) | 1974–1980 | |
		In-creased	De-creased		In-crease	De-crease
Public						
Research universities						
Total faculty	(33)	88	a	(31)	39	10
Tenured	(36)	86	a	(36)	39	3
Nontenured	(36)	69	6	(36)	25	19
Research	(30)	57	3	(30)	20	3
Part-time	(34)	41	6	(34)	21	12
Other doctoral						
Total faculty	(32)	81	6	(32)	28	16
Tenured	(36)	81	a	(36)	41	9
Nontenured	(30)	57	30	(30)	33	23
Research	(29)	17	3	(29)	10	7
Part-time	(32)	41	19	(31)	23	16
Comprehensive colleges & universities						
Total faculty	(168)	74	13	(163)	39	14
Tenured	(170)	81	1	(166)	49	5
Nontenured	(169)	57	24	(163)	34	25
Research	(72)	22	4	(73)	18	3
Part-time	(168)	48	10	(161)	32	11
Liberal arts colleges						
Total faculty	(20)	90	5	(20)	80	5
Tenured	(20)	95	a	(19)	79	5
Nontenured	(20)	80	15	(19)	74	5
Research	(2)	b	b	(2)	b	b
Part-time	(17)	77	6	(17)	77	17
Two-year institutions						
Total faculty	(324)	85	3	(308)	55	4
Tenured	(250)	79	2	(243)	58	3
Nontenured	(273)	61	11	(270)	39	13
Research	(46)	17	2	(43)	9	2
Part-time	(318)	77	5	(311)	63	3
Professional schools						
Total faculty	(16)	62	19	(16)	63	a
Tenured	(15)	67	7	(14)	b	b
Nontenured	(14)	b	b	(7)	b	b
Research	(8)	b	b	(9)	b	b
Part-time	(14)	b	b	(14)	b	b

Cont'd.

Table 45. Change in number of faculty, actual 1968–1974 and anticipated 1974–1980, by Carnegie type and control (by percentages of responding institutions) (Cont'd.)

Type of faculty	(N)	1968–1974		(N)	1974–1980	
		In- creased	De- creased		In- crease	De- crease
Private						
Research universities						
Total faculty	(19)	58	26	(18)	11	17
Tenured	(21)	76	a	(19)	5	5
Nontenured	(21)	43	38	(19)	16	16
Research	(17)	29	6	(16)	13	a
Part-time	(18)	39	28	(16)	6	6
Other doctoral						
Total faculty	(18)	61	17	(17)	12	11
Tenured	(18)	61	11	(17)	49	5
Nontenured	(17)	53	18	(16)	13	50
Research	(12)	b	b	(12)	b	b
Part-time	(18)	39	17	(18)	22	11
Comprehensive colleges & universities						
Total faculty	(79)	56	32	(76)	11	21
Tenured	(80)	71	5	(78)	40	10
Nontenured	(81)	40	38	(77)	13	36
Research	(19)	11	5	(19)	5	5
Part-time	(80)	41	21	(77)	30	23
Liberal arts colleges						
Total faculty	(296)	48	22	(282)	22	16
Tenured	(280)	55	8	(271)	40	7
Nontenured	(283)	33	33	(273)	19	30
Research	(59)	10	14	(58)	14	5
Part-time	(293)	38	13	(279)	33	11
Two-year institutions						
Total faculty	(74)	34	26	(70)	37	4
Tenured	(38)	45	5	(36)	28	8
Nontenured	(58)	28	28	(55)	24	13
Research	(10)	b	b	(10)	b	b
Part-time	(65)	43	8	(66)	44	9
Professional schools						
Total faculty	(85)	71	11	(84)	44	5
Tenured	(61)	46	8	(61)	34	10
Nontenured	(58)	64	14	(55)	41	9
Research	(8)	b	b	(9)	b	b
Part-time	(75)	49	9	(73)	32	8

a No observations.

b Not calculated; base less than 15 cases.

Note: "Increase" and "decrease" denote changes of more than 5 percent.

Table 46. Change in number of tenured, nontenured, and total faculty, by change in FTE enrollment, Carnegie type, and control, 1968–1974 (in percentages of responding institutions)

Change in FTE enrollment	Total faculty			Nontenured faculty			Tenured faculty		
	(N)	Increased	Decreased	(N)	Increased	Decreased	(N)	Increased	Decreased
Research and doctoral universities									
Public:									
Increased	(47)	92	a	(48)	85	a	(46)	78	7
Little change, decreased	(19)	71	6	(19)	84	a	(19)	26	42
Private:									
Increased	(18)	72	22	(18)	89	6	(17)	65	29
Little change, decreased	(19)	47	21	(20)	50	5	(20)	30	30
Comprehensive colleges & universities									
Public:									
Increased	(114)	94	2	(115)	90	a	(115)	72	15
Little change	(26)	42	12	(26)	65	4	(26)	27	27
Decreased	(22)	18	68	(23)	57	a	(23)	13	74
Private:									
Increased	(32)	81	9	(32)	75	3	(32)	56	19
Little change	(22)	59	18	(24)	63	8	(24)	42	29
Decreased	(23)	13	78	(22)	73	5	(23)	9	78

Liberal arts, public & private									
Increased	(134)	75	8	(127)	70	4	(130)	55	16
Little change	(91)	44	11	(88)	56	2	(86)	27	29
Decreased	(76)	8	60	(72)	39	19	(74)	11	64
Two-year institutions									
Public:									
Increased	(267)	94	[b]	(204)	85	[a]	(232)	69	7
Little change, decreased	(50)	38	20	(42)	48	12	(38)	13	34
Private:									
Increased	(27)	63	7	(15)	53	[a]	(22)	50	5
Little change, decreased	(39)	13	36	(23)	39	9	(33)	12	46
Professional schools, public & private									
Increased	(54)	91	4	(36)	64	3	(43)	86	7
Little change, decreased	(38)	34	26	(34)	35	15	(31)	29	32

[a] No observations.

[b] Less than .5 percent.

Note: "Increase" and "decrease" in enrollment denote changes of more than 10 percent. "Increase" and "decrease" in number of faculty denote changes of more than 5 percent.

Table 47. Change in number of faculty, by change in real expenditures per FTE student, Carnegie type, and control, 1968–1974 (in percentages of responding institutions)

Change in expenditures per FTE student	Change in number of total faculty		
	(N)	Increased	Decreased
Research & doctoral universities			
Public:			
Increased	(20)	90	a
Little change, decreased	(40)	85	5
Private:			
Increased	(15)	53	27
Little change, decreased	(17)	59	24
Comprehensive colleges & universities			
Public:			
Increased	(73)	82	4
Little change, decreased	(77)	68	18
Private:			
Increased	(42)	62	31
Little change, decreased	(26)	50	31
Liberal arts, public & private			
Increased	(152)	51	24
Little change, decreased	(115)	51	21
Two-year institutions			
Public:			
Increased	(153)	88	2
Little change, decreased	(134)	83	4
Private:			
Increased	(43)	37	28
Little change, decreased	(20)	25	20
Professional schools, public & private			
Increased	(58)	76	14
Little change, decreased	(27)	59	4

[a] No observations.

Note: "Increase" and "decrease" in expenditures denote changes of more than 10 percent. "Increase" and "decrease" in number of faculty denote changes of more than 5 percent.

Table 48. Change in number of faculty, actual 1968–1974 and anticipated 1974–1980, by change in FTE enrollment and expenditures per FTE student 1968–1974, Carnegie type, and control (in percentages of responding institutions)

Change in FTE enrollment and expenditures per FTE student, 1968–1974	Total instructional faculty					
	1968–1974			1974–1980		
	(N)	In-creased	De-creased	(N)	In-crease	De-crease
Public universities & comprehensives						
Increased enrollment and:						
Increased expenditures	(68)	97	a	(66)	53	8
Little change, decreased expenditures	(78)	90	3	(75)	41	5
Little change, decreased enrollment and:						
Increased expenditures	(22)	50	14	(23)	13	35
Little change, decreased expenditures	(36)	39	36	(33)	6	27
Private universities & comprehensives						
Increased enrollment and:						
Increased expenditures	(23)	83	9	(23)	9	17
Little change, decreased expenditures	(20)	80	15	(19)	11	21
Little change, decreased enrollment and:						
Increased expenditures	(33)	42	46	(31)	7	26
Little change, decreased expenditures	(23)	30	39	(22)	18	14
Private liberal arts						
Increased enrollment and:						
Increased expenditures	(56)	80	9	(51)	29	12
Little change, decreased expenditures	(45)	69	11	(43)	42	5
Little change, and:						
Increased expenditures	(40)	53	10	(38)	8	21
Little change, decreased expenditures	(35)	37	14	(36)	8	11
Decreased enrollment and:						
Increased expenditures	(45)	4	62	(43)	19	21
Little change, decreased expenditures	(20)	5	65	(18)	22	17
Public two-year institutions						
Increased enrollment and:						
Increased expenditures	(130)	95	a	(123)	60	2
Little change, decreased expenditures	(108)	92	1	(103)	61	5
Little change, decreased enrollment and:						
Increased expenditures	(20)	35	15	(20)	30	5
Little change, decreased expenditures	(23)	44	17	(20)	10	a

Cont'd.

Table 48. Change in number of faculty, actual 1968–1974 and anticipated 1974–1980, by change in FTE enrollment and expenditures per FTE student 1968–1974, Carnegie type, and control (in percentages of responding institutions) (Cont'd.)

	Tenured faculty					
	1968–1974			1974–1980		
Change in FTE enrollment and expenditures per FTE student, 1968–1974	(N)	In-creased	De-creased	(N)	In-crease	De-crease
Public universities & comprehensives						
Increased enrollment and:						
Increased expenditures	(70)	89	a	(68)	52	6
Little change, decreased expenditures	(78)	89	a	(77)	53	1
Little change, decreased enrollment and:						
Increased expenditures	(22)	77	a	(23)	44	4
Little change, decreased expenditures	(38)	66	a	(35)	23	9
Private universities & comprehensives						
Increased enrollment and:						
Increased expenditures	(24)	71	8	(24)	38	13
Little change, decreased expenditures	(20)	90	a	(18)	28	6
Little change, decreased enrollment and:						
Increased expenditures	(35)	60	9	(33)	33	6
Little change, decreased expenditures	(24)	58	4	(24)	38	8
Private liberal arts						
Increased enrollment and:						
Increased expenditures	(52)	64	8	(49)	55	6
Little change, decreased expenditures	(44)	64	2	(41)	56	12
Little change, and:						
Increased expenditures	(37)	57	a	(36)	33	a
Little change, decreased expenditures	(36)	58	6	(36)	36	6
Decreased enrollment and:						
Increased expenditures	(42)	45	17	(42)	33	12
Little change, decreased expenditures	(19)	26	21	(19)	32	5
Public two-year institutions						
Increased enrollment and:						
Increased expenditures	(95)	92	a	(91)	68	4
Little change, decreased expenditures	(83)	81	a	(81)	61	3
Little change, decreased enrollment and:						
Increased expenditures	(17)	53	6	(17)	47	a
Little change, decreased expenditures	(21)	43	14	(21)	19	5

Table 48. Change in number of faculty, actual 1968–1974 and anticipated 1974–1980, by change in FTE enrollment and expenditures per FTE student 1968–1974, Carnegie type, and control (in percentages of responding institutions) (Cont'd.)

Change in FTE enrollment and expenditures per FTE student, 1968–1974	Nontenured faculty					
	1968–1974			1974–1980		
	(N)	In-creased	De-creased	(N)	In-crease	De-crease
Public universities & comprehensives						
Increased enrollment and:						
Increased expenditures	(68)	71	16	(66)	44	24
Little change, decreased expenditures	(78)	76	10	(76)	41	13
Little change, decreased enrollment and:						
Increased expenditures	(22)	23	46	(23)	9	52
Little change, decreased expenditures	(38)	24	42	(35)	6	29
Private universities & comprehensives						
Increased enrollment and:						
Increased expenditures	(23)	48	26	(23)	26	35
Little change, decreased expenditures	(20)	85	15	(17)	12	35
Little change, decreased enrollment and:						
Increased expenditures	(35)	31	46	(33)	6	39
Little change, decreased expenditures	(24)	17	50	(24)	13	29
Private liberal arts						
Increased enrollment and:						
Increased expenditures	(52)	58	17	(49)	22	22
Little change, decreased expenditures	(44)	48	23	(40)	40	23
Little change, and:						
Increased expenditures	(37)	38	19	(36)	6	39
Little change, decreased expenditures	(34)	18	41	(34)	3	47
Decreased enrollment and:						
Increased expenditures	(43)	14	67	(42)	19	33
Little change, decreased expenditures	(19)	5	68	(19)	16	26
Public two-year institutions						
Increased enrollment and:						
Increased expenditures	(111)	68	10	(107)	38	12
Little change, decreased expenditures	(98)	71	5	(96)	47	14
Little change, decreased enrollment and:						
Increased expenditures	(16)	6	25	(18)	17	17
Little change, decreased expenditures	(18)	17	39	(19)	11	21

[a]No observations.

Note: "Increase" and "decrease" in enrollment and expenditures denote changes of over 10 percent. "Increase" and "decrease" in number of faculty denote changes of over 5 percent.

Table 49. Percentages of institutions reporting an increase in specified personnel policies, actual 1968–1974 and anticipated 1974–1980, by Carnegie type and control

Carnegie type and control	Efforts to evaluate faculty teaching			Efforts to retrain faculty			Incentives for early retirement		
	(N)	1968–1974	1974–1980	(N)	1968–1974	1974–1980	(N)	1968–1974	1974–1980
Public									
Research universities	(36,36)	75	75	(36,36)	6	50	(36,36)	19	78
Other doctoral	(32,32)	63	84	(32,32)	13	56	(32,32)	22	75
Comprehensive	(172,171)	67	85	(171,169)	16	64	(172,170)	19	60
Liberal arts	(20,19)	55	84	(20,19)	10	68	(20,19)	5	53
Two-year	(330,326)	69	84	(327,322)	26	54	(321,316)	15	37
Professional	(17,17)	47	59	(16,16)	19	38	(17,17)	6	29
Private									
Research universities	(21,20)	43	65	(21,20)	10	25	(21,20)	38	60
Other doctoral	(19,19)	79	90	(19,18)	5	72	(19,18)	32	56
Comprehensive	(81,81)	68	84	(80,80)	18	55	(81,81)	7	51
Liberal arts	(308,303)	75	82	(305,302)	28	54	(301,298)	9	41
Two-year	(71,68)	61	79	(69,67)	26	48	(64,62)	6	15
Professional	(87,85)	66	81	(84,82)	13	28	(83,81)	7	21

Table 50. Change in efforts to retrain faculty, 1968–1974 and 1974–1980, by change in FTE enrollment, 1968–1974, Carnegie type, and control (in percentages of responding institutions)

Change in FTE enrollment, 1968–1974		1968–1974			1974–1980	
	(N)	In-creased	Little change	(N)	In-crease	De-crease
Research & doctoral universities						
Public:						
Increased	(48)	8	92	(48)	50	50
Little change, decreased	(19)	10	90	(19)	63	37
Private:						
Increased	(18)	11	89	(17)	47	53
Little change, decreased	(21)	5	95	(20)	50	50
Comprehensive colleges & universities						
Public:						
Increased	(115)	14	86	(113)	61	39
Little change	(27)	15	85	(27)	67	33
Decreased	(23)	26	74	(23)	74	26
Private:						
Increased	(33)	24	76	(33)	55	45
Little change	(23)	13	87	(23)	61	39
Decreased	(23)	13	87	(23)	52	48
Liberal arts, public & private						
Increased	(135)	24	76	(133)	56	44
Little change	(93)	27	73	(92)	54	45
Decreased	(83)	30	70	(81)	52	47
Two-year institutions						
Public:						
Increased	(265)	27	73	(263)	55	45
Little change, decreased	(53)	19	81	(49)	47	53
Private:						
Increased	(23)	35	61	(23)	52	44
Little change, decreased	(39)	23	77	(36)	50	50
Professional schools, public & private						
Increased	(53)	13	83	(53)	30	68
Little change, decreased	(38)	16	84	(38)	32	68

Note: "Increase" and "decrease" in enrollment denote changes of more than 10 percent. "Little change" denotes a change of up to ± 10 percent.

Table 51. Percentages of institutions reporting "extensive" and "some" change in emphasis on active recruitment of various types of students, actual 1968–1974 and anticipated 1974–1980, by Carnegie type and control

	1968–1974			1974–1980		
Type of students	(N)	Exten-sive	Some	(N)	Exten-sive	Some
Public						
Research & doctoral universities						
Traditional students	(68)	29	56	(66)	52	41
Ethnic minorities	(69)	64	33	(67)	66	33
Evening students	(59)	12	49	(60)	43	47
Low-income students	(68)	35	49	(65)	46	48
Adults over 22	(67)	10	57	(65)	55	36
Transfer students	(67)	24	54	(65)	46	43
Off-campus students	(60)	18	53	(61)	49	36
Early admissions from h.s.	(65)	10	50	(63)	19	59
Previous dropouts	(61)	3	30	(61)	18	41
Comprehensive colleges & universities						
Traditional students	(168)	65	29	(164)	74	23
Ethnic minorities	(169)	66	31	(165)	67	31
Evening students	(160)	42	42	(157)	77	20
Low-income students	(162)	49	39	(157)	59	34
Adults over 22	(164)	38	44	(158)	77	21
Transfer students	(168)	51	44	(163)	71	26
Off-campus students	(141)	38	40	(139)	71	23
Early admissions from h.s.	(153)	15	53	(147)	39	46
Previous dropouts	(157)	13	35	(148)	34	45
Liberal arts colleges						
Traditional students	(20)	60	25	(20)	70	30
Ethnic minorities	(19)	42	37	(19)	48	47
Evening students	(18)	22	50	(18)	61	22
Low-income students	(20)	40	40	(20)	55	30
Adults over 22	(19)	32	37	(19)	84	0
Transfer students	(20)	40	40	(20)	75	15
Off-campus students	(19)	16	53	(19)	47	32
Early admissions from h.s.	(17)	12	53	(18)	44	45
Previous dropouts	(18)	6	44	(18)	22	45
Two-year institutions						
Traditional students	(326)	59	36	(319)	66	31
Ethnic minorities	(324)	52	40	(317)	62	33
Evening students	(324)	67	27	(316)	85	13
Low-income students	(324)	56	38	(317)	68	29
Adults over 22	(327)	64	31	(320)	84	14

Table 51. Percentages of institutions reporting "extensive" and "some" change in emphasis on active recruitment of various types of students, actual 1968–1974 and anticipated 1974–1980, by Carnegie type and control (Cont'd.)

	1968–1974			1974–1980		
Type of students	*(N)*	*Exten-sive*	*Some*	*(N)*	*Exten-sive*	*Some*
Public (Cont'd.)						
Transfer students	(300)	26	46	(394)	36	43
Off-campus students	(300)	55	33	(296)	77	19
Early admissions from h.s.	(312)	19	57	(306)	43	45
Previous dropouts	(323)	28	47	(316)	52	37
Professional schools						
Traditional students	(16)	37	44	(17)	41	47
Ethnic minorities	(17)	53	35	(17)	41	59
Evening students	(6)	a	a	(6)	a	a
Low-income students	(16)	25	31	(16)	19	50
Adults over 22	(11)	a	a	(11)	a	a
Transfer students	(17)	18	35	(17)	35	30
Off-campus students	(8)	a	a	(9)	a	a
Early admissions from h.s.	(13)	a	a	(14)	a	a
Previous dropouts	(10)	a	a	(10)	a	a
Private						
Research & doctoral universities						
Traditional students	(40)	75	23	(39)	82	18
Ethnic minorities	(39)	67	33	(39)	67	32
Evening students	(32)	22	38	(31)	45	26
Low-income students	(39)	23	64	(39)	21	72
Adults over 22	(36)	17	36	(36)	45	33
Transfer students	(40)	58	30	(39)	82	13
Off-campus students	(30)	13	40	(29)	34	34
Early admissions from h.s.	(37)	19	51	(36)	34	44
Previous dropouts	(34)	b	26	(37)	13	41
Comprehensive colleges & universities						
Traditional students	(82)	82	18	(81)	75	24
Ethnic minorities	(80)	55	38	(79)	39	55
Evening students	(72)	31	43	(70)	64	29
Low-income students	(81)	33	56	(81)	25	63
Adults over 22	(80)	30	49	(80)	68	27
Transfer students	(82)	57	34	(82)	74	22
Off-campus students	(64)	25	44	(63)	45	41
Early admissions from h.s.	(80)	15	59	(80)	31	58
Previous dropouts	(76)	4	34	(75)	13	48

Cont'd.

Table 51. Percentages of institutions reporting "extensive" and "some" change in emphasis on active recruitment of various types of students, actual 1968– 1974 and anticipated 1974–1980, by Carnegie type and control (Cont'd.)

Type of students	1968–1974			1974–1980		
	(N)	Exten-sive	Some	(N)	Exten-sive	Some
Private (Cont'd.)						
Liberal arts colleges						
Traditional students	(308)	75	22	(299)	77	21
Ethnic minorities	(308)	44	47	(298)	41	54
Evening students	(224)	24	39	(218)	53	29
Low-income students	(305)	28	54	(294)	28	57
Adults over 22	(298)	24	39	(287)	53	32
Transfer students	(310)	45	47	(301)	74	24
Off-campus students	(231)	24	37	(226)	44	35
Early admissions from h.s.	(299)	8	57	(290)	29	55
Previous dropouts	(263)	6	34	(254)	23	35
Two-year institutions						
Traditional students	(73)	70	25	(68)	72	25
Ethnic minorities	(73)	36	53	(67)	37	55
Evening students	(62)	42	31	(60)	65	27
Low-income students	(71)	37	52	(65)	39	52
Adults over 22	(71)	35	41	(66)	58	30
Transfer students	(63)	16	43	(58)	17	55
Off-campus students	(51)	33	37	(51)	51	31
Early admissions from h.s.	(72)	19	46	(67)	36	46
Previous dropouts	(61)	17	44	(57)	17	53
Professional schools						
Traditional students	(73)	49	45	(73)	58	42
Ethnic minorities	(77)	25	56	(73)	37	49
Evening students	(55)	23	44	(53)	40	49
Low-income students	(69)	15	58	(69)	20	62
Adults over 22	(65)	26	43	(63)	44	35
Transfer students	(71)	25	30	(69)	38	30
Off-campus students	(54)	19	44	(52)	33	46
Early admissions from h.s.	(44)	11	30	(44)	16	64
Previous dropouts	(53)	4	30	(52)	15	35

[a]Not calculated; base less than 15 cases.

[b]Less than .5 percent.

Table 52. Change in FTE enrollment and in expenditures, by change in emphasis on active recruitment of five types of students, Carnegie type, and control, 1968–1974 (in percentages of responding institutions)

Type of students and change in emphasis on recruitment	FTE enrollment			Expenditures per FTE student		
	(N)	In-creased	De-creased	(N)	In-creased	De-creased
Early admissions from high school						
Public						
Universities & comprehensive colleges						
Extensive	(26)	65	19	(26)	50	8
Some	(107)	74	10	(106)	44	7
Very little	(74)	62	8	(70)	41	11
Two-year						
Extensive	(55)	87	5	(54)	63	9
Some	(169)	82	7	(159)	51	6
Very little	(70)	83	4	(70)	50	6
Private						
Universities & comprehensive colleges						
Extensive	(18)	45	45	(14)	a	a
Some	(62)	45	23	(61)	53	7
Very little	(31)	39	23	(29)	66	b
Liberal arts						
Extensive	(23)	48	35	(21)	76	b
Some	(156)	39	30	(150)	63	3
Very little	(95)	46	20	(85)	44	5
Traditional students						
Public						
Universities & comprehensive colleges						
Extensive	(121)	67	16	(117)	56	3
Some	(82)	71	5	(76)	29	16
Very little	(21)	76	5	(20)	30	15
Two-year						
Extensive	(185)	82	9	(171)	54	5
Some, very little	(123)	86	1	(117)	51	8
Private						
Universities & comprehensive colleges						
Extensive	(93)	45	28	(82)	61	5
Some, very little	(23)	39	13	(24)	46	4

Cont'd.

Table 52. Change in FTE enrollment and in expenditures, by change in emphasis on active recruitment of five types of students, Carnegie type, and control, 1968–1974 (in percentages of responding institutions) (Cont'd.)

Type of students and change in emphasis on recruitment	FTE enrollment			Expenditures per FTE student		
	(N)	In-creased	De-creased	(N)	In-creased	De-creased
Liberal arts						
Extensive	(212)	42	26	(198)	61	4
Some, very little	(70)	37	33	(62)	47	5
Ethnic minorities						
Public						
Universities & comprehensive colleges						
Extensive	(148)	71	10	(142)	44	10
Some, very little	(78)	67	11	(71)	44	7
Two-year						
Extensive	(165)	88	4	(147)	53	7
Some	(120)	82	7	(118)	53	5
Very little	(21)	62	14	(22)	55	5
Private						
Universities & comprehensive colleges						
Extensive	(61)	59	6	(63)	59	5
Some, very little	(37)	57	5	(40)	53	5
Liberal arts						
Extensive	(108)	57	6	(115)	56	6
Some	(116)	59	2	(121)	58	3
Very little	(22)	68	b	(23)	67	b
Adult students over 22						
Public						
Universities & comprehensive colleges						
Extensive	(66)	71	14	(65)	48	9
Some	(106)	69	8	(98)	43	10
Very little	(48)	69	11	(45)	44	7
Two-year						
Extensive	(202)	85	6	(187)	52	8
Some, very little	(107)	82	7	(102)	54	4

Table 52. Change in FTE enrollment and in expenditures, by change in emphasis on active recruitment of five types of students, Carnegie type, and control, 1968–1974 (in percentages of responding institutions) (Cont'd.)

Type of students and change in emphasis on recruitment	FTE enrollment			Expenditures per FTE student		
	(N)	In-creased	De-creased	(N)	In-creased	De-creased
Private						
Universities & comprehensive colleges						
Extensive	(29)	55	24	(22)	68	5
Some	(49)	41	35	(47)	55	5
Very little	(33)	39	15	(33)	52	6
Liberal arts						
Extensive	(65)	45	34	(60)	53	8
Some	(107)	42	30	(97)	65	2
Very little	(102)	41	23	(92)	54	3
Transfer students						
Public						
Universities & comprehensive colleges						
Extensive	(98)	63	18	(94)	51	5
Some	(103)	76	4	(99)	41	11
Very little	(22)	64	9	(19)	26	16
Two-year						
Extensive	(76)	78	13	(69)	55	6
Some	(128)	78	13	(126)	52	7
Very little	(80)	81	5	(75)	49	3
Private						
Universities & comprehensive colleges						
Extensive	(67)	48	24	(59)	53	7
Some, very little	(49)	39	27	(47)	64	2
Liberal arts						
Extensive	(128)	45	26	(120)	62	6
Some	(132)	38	30	(121)	58	3
Very little	(24)	46	29	(21)	38	b

[a] Not calculated; base less than 15 cases.

[b] No observations.

Note: "Increase" and "decrease" in enrollment and expenditures denote changes of more than 10 percent.

Table 53. Extent of change in use of market survey and needs analysis by change in emphasis on active recruitment of five types of students, Carnegie type, and control, 1968–1974 (in percentages of responding institutions)

Type of students and change in emphasis on recruitment	(N)	Change in use of market survey		
		Extensive	Some	Very little
Traditional students				
Public				
Universities & comprehensive colleges				
Extensive	(121)	8	59	33
Some	(85)	7	49	44
Very little	(19)	11	26	63
Two-year				
Extensive	(181)	23	53	24
Some, very little	(125)	17	57	26
Private				
Universities & comprehensive colleges				
Extensive	(95)	19	47	34
Some, very little	(24)	a	38	62
Liberal arts				
Extensive	(215)	12	44	44
Some, very little	(63)	6	46	48
Total	(1,098)	14	48	38
Ethnic minorities				
Public				
Universities & comprehensive colleges				
Extensive	(149)	11	48	41
Some, very little	(78)	3	61	36
Two-year				
Extensive	(160)	23	58	19
Some	(122)	16	52	32
Very little	(22)	18	50	32
Private				
Universities & comprehensive colleges				
Extensive	(69)	19	49	32
Some, very little	(47)	11	38	51
Liberal arts				
Extensive	(121)	13	38	49
Some	(130)	9	52	39
Very little	(26)	8	42	50
Total	(1,098)	14	48	38

Table 53. Extent of change in use of market survey and needs analysis by change in emphasis on active recruitment of five types of students, Carnegie type, and control, 1968–1974 (in percentages of responding institutions) (Cont'd.)

| Type of students and change in emphasis on recruitment | (N) | Change in use of market survey | | |
		Extensive	*Some*	*Very little*
Adults over 22				
Public				
Universities & comprehensive colleges				
Extensive	(64)	11	59	30
Some	(108)	7	55	38
Very little	(48)	8	35	57
Two-year				
Extensive	(198)	24	56	20
Some, very little	(108)	13	53	34
Private				
Universities & comprehensive colleges				
Extensive	(29)	21	48	31
Some	(52)	16	42	42
Very little	(33)	8	46	46
Liberal arts				
Extensive	(65)	17	54	29
Some	(108)	12	45	43
Very little	(97)	4	40	56
Total	(1,098)	14	48	38
Transfer students				
Public				
Universities & comprehensive colleges				
Extensive	(97)	8	55	37
Some	(105)	9	52	39
Very little	(22)	5	41	54
Two-year				
Extensive	(71)	21	61	18
Some	(129)	17	59	24
Very little	(81)	16	48	36
Private				
Universities & comprehensive colleges				
Extensive	(69)	22	48	30
Some, very little	(50)	6	42	52
Liberal arts				
Extensive	(127)	14	48	38
Some	(131)	8	45	47
Very little	(21)	[a]	33	67
Total	(1,098)	14	48	38

Cont'd.

Table 53. Extent of change in use of market survey and needs analysis by change in emphasis on active recruitment of five types of students, Carnegie type, and control, 1968–1974 (in percentages of responding institutions) (Cont'd.)

Type of students and change in emphasis on recruitment	(N)	Change in use of market survey		
		Extensive	Some	Very little
Early admissions from high school				
Public				
Universities & comprehensive colleges				
Extensive	(28)	21	61	18
Some	(111)	6	55	39
Very little	(69)	4	50	46
Two-year				
Extensive	(55)	33	45	22
Some	(167)	19	56	25
Very little	(70)	11	60	29
Private				
Universities & comprehensive colleges				
Extensive	(18)	28	50	22
Some	(64)	16	48	38
Very little	(32)	6	38	56
Liberal arts				
Extensive	(21)	14	62	24
Some	(157)	12	47	41
Very little	(92)	7	39	54
Total	(1,098)	14	48	38

ᵃ No observations.

Table 54. Percentages of institutions reporting "extensive" or "some" modification of admissions standards to increase enrollments, actual 1968–1974 and anticipated 1974–1980, by Carnegie type and control

Carnegie type and control	(N)	To increase undergraduate enrollment		
		1968–1974	1974–1980	Percentage point change
Public				
Research & doctoral	(64,63)	30	41	11
Comprehensive	(165,157)	45	46	1
Liberal arts	(19,19)	42	32	−10
Two-year	(291,277)	44	43	−1
Professional	(15,14)	33	a	a
Total Public	(554,530)	43	43	0
Private				
Research & doctoral	(39,38)	33	26	−7
Comprehensive	(81,80)	37	40	3
Liberal arts	(308,287)	41	41	0
Two-year	(71,66)	52	44	−8
Professional	(53,51)	26	25	−1
Total private	(552,522)	40	39	−1

		To increase graduate enrollment		
		1968–1974	1974–1980	Percentage point change
Total public	(235,225)	19	30	11
Total private	(193,192)	18	25	7

		To increase professional enrollment		
		1968–1974	1974–1980	Percentage point change
Total public	(154,156)	14	26	12
Total private	(157,154)	15	19	4

a Not calculated; base less than 15 cases.

Table 55. Percentages of institutions reporting "extensive" or "some" modification of admissions standards to increase undergraduate enrollments, 1968–1974, by change in FTE enrollment and expenditures, selected Carnegie categories, and control

Change in FTE enrollment	*(N)*	*Percentages of institutions*
Public		
Universities & comprehensive colleges		
Increased	(143)	40
Little change, decreased	(58)	47
Two-year institutions		
Increased	(213)	46
Little change, decreased	(41)	46
Private		
Universities & comprehensive colleges		
Increased	(43)	35
Little change, decreased	(59)	41
Liberal arts		
Increased	(105)	36
Little change, decreased	(144)	46

Change in expenditures per FTE student		
Public		
Universities & comprehensive colleges		
Increased	(90)	52
Little change, decreased	(111)	33
Two-year institutions		
Increased	(136)	49
Little change, decreased	(118)	42
Private		
Universities & comprehensive colleges		
Increased	(58)	36
Little change, decreased	(44)	41
Liberal arts		
Increased	(146)	45
Little change, decreased	(103)	37

Note: "Increase" and "decrease" in enrollment and expenditures denote changes of more than 10 percent.

Table 56. Percentages of institutions reporting "extensive" or "some" modification of admissions standards to increase under-graduate enrollment, by change in emphasis on recruitment of five types of students, Carnegie type, and control, 1968–1974

Change in emphasis on recruitment	(N)	Traditional students	(N)	Ethnic minorities	(N)	Adults over 22	(N)	Transfer students	(N)	Early admits from h.s.
Universities & comprehensive colleges										
Public										
Extensive	(128)	46	(150)	47	(68)	47	(100)	51	(27)	48
Some	(80)	36	(79)	29[a]	(105)	44	(106)	35	(113)	50
Very little	(20)	30			(51)	25	(22)	27	(73)	29
Private										
Extensive	(95)	39	(68)	36	(30)	47	(68)	44	(18)	44
Some	(25)	24[a]	(49)	35[a]	(51)	43	(52)	25[a]	(65)	41
Very little					(33)	21			(32)	25
Private liberal arts										
Extensive	(230)	42	(133)	49	(71)	63	(139)	47	(25)	48
Some	(74)	36[a]	(142)	32	(114)	37	(144)	35	(166)	45
Very little			(29)	48	(110)	34	(23)	48	(104)	33
Public two-year institutions										
Extensive	(176)	46	(149)	46	(194)	44	(68)	56	(56)	55
Some	(112)	41[a]	(114)	43	(95)	44[a]	(119)	47	(154)	45
Very little			(22)	46			(77)	30	(69)	35

[a] Institutions with "some" or "very little" recruitment are combined because numbers are small in "very little" category.

Table 57. Percentages of institutions reporting increases in instructional programs designed to serve "new students," by type of student program, actual 1968–1974 and anticipated 1974–1980, Carnegie type, and control

Types of "new student" programs and Carnegie type	Public				Private			
	(N)	1968–1974	1974–1980	Percentage point change	(N)	1968–1974	1974–1980	Percentage point change
Programs for ethnic minorities								
Research & doctoral	(66,67)	71	39	−32	(37,36)	62	17	−45
Comprehensive	(168,163)	58	40	−18	(78,78)	49	19	−30
Liberal arts	(20,19)	45	53	8	(284,263)	43	25	−18
Two-year	(309,299)	51	41	−10	(62,57)	31	33	2
Professional	(11,10)	a	a	a	(59,62)	29	24	−5
Programs for adults over 22								
Research & doctoral	(65,66)	51	80	29	(35,32)	34	69	35
Comprehensive	(167,164)	54	82	28	(73,74)	67	78	11
Liberal arts	(20,19)	50	79	29	(268,253)	48	74	26
Two-year	(317,310)	73	80	7	(64,59)	44	63	19
Professional	(7,6)	a	a	a	(62,63)	37	46	9

Programs for evening students								
Research & doctoral	(61,63)	56	76	20	(31,29)	35	48	13
Comprehensive	(165,163)	55	79	24	(71,70)	52	66	14
Liberal arts	(18,18)	61	83	22	(213,209)	51	75	24
Two-year	(322,312)	77	81	4	(55,53)	58	83	25
Professional	(7,5)	a	a	a	(56,55)	52	51	−1
Programs for off-campus students								
Research & doctoral	(61,63)	64	78	14	(23,23)	48	61	13
Comprehensive	(150,150)	63	83	20	(59,59)	63	66	3
Liberal arts	(16,15)	44	80	36	(182,182)	53	70	17
Two-year	(303,298)	73	82	9	(35,36)	46	81	35
Professional	(8,7)	a	a	a	(47,51)	62	63	1

[a]Not calculated; base less than 15 cases.

Table 58. Percentages of institutions reporting increases in instructional programs designed to serve "new students," by change in FTE enrollment, Carnegie type, and control, 1968–1974

Change in FTE enrollment		Increase in programs						
	(N)	*Ethnic minority*	*(N)*	*Adult over 22*	*(N)*	*Off-campus*	*(N)*	*Evening*
Research & doctoral universities								
Public:								
Increased	(46)	65	(45)	49	(44)	64	(41)	59
Little change, decreased	(19)	84	(19)	58	(16)	69	(19)	53
Private:								
Increased	(17)	77	(16)	50	(9)	a	(11)	a
Little change, decreased	(19)	47	(18)	22	(14)	a	(19)	26
Comprehensive colleges & universities								
Public:								
Increased	(113)	66	(113)	61	(101)	66	(111)	58
Little change	(26)	39	(25)	32	(22)	64	(25)	48
Decreased	(23)	52	(23)	52	(23)	57	(23)	52
Private:								
Increased	(30)	53	(29)	72	(24)	67	(29)	66
Little change	(23)	52	(22)	59	(17)	65	(20)	50
Decreased	(23)	39	(20)	65	(16)	50	(20)	30
Liberal arts, public & private								
Increased	(130)	45	(124)	48	(89)	55	(107)	51
Little change	(84)	48	(78)	41	(49)	49	(56)	52
Decreased	(77)	34	(74)	55	(52)	54	(62)	50
Two-year institutions								
Public:								
Increased	(255)	55	(259)	75	(249)	76	(265)	80
Little change, decreased	(48)	40	(51)	61	(47)	57	(50)	60
Private:								
Increased	(23)	44	(24)	54	(17)	53	(21)	67
Little change, decreased	(34)	21	(34)	29	(16)	38	(28)	46

Table 58. Percentages of institutions reporting increases in instructional programs designed to serve "new students," by change in FTE enrollment, Carnegie type, and control, 1968–1974 (Cont'd.)

				Increase in programs				
Change in FTE enrollment	*(N)*	*Ethnic minor-ity*	*(N)*	*Adult over 22*	*(N)*	*Off-cam-pus*	*(N)*	*Eve-ning*
Professional schools, public & private								
Increased	(34)	27	(30)	57	(26)	77	(32)	63
Little change, decreased	(31)	39	(34)	29	(26)	58	(27)	37

ᵃ Not calculated; base less than 15 cases.

Note: "Increase" and "decrease" in enrollment denote changes of more than 10 percent. "Little change" denotes a change of up to ±10 percent.

Table 59. Change in number of instructional programs, by level of program, actual 1968–1974 and anticipated 1974–1980, Carnegie type, and control (in percentages of responding institutions)

Level of program	(N)	1968–1974 In- creased	De- creased	Net in- crease or de- crease	(N)	1974–1980 In- crease	De- crease	Net in- crease or de- crease
Undergraduate level programs								
Research & doctoral universities								
Public	(66)	68	5	63	(67)	12	16	−4
Private	(38)	34	8	26	(36)	14	19	−5
Comprehensive colleges & universities								
Public	(171)	74	1	74	(168)	38	8	30
Private	(81)	44	4	41	(80)	11	15	−4
Liberal arts colleges								
Public	(20)	75	5	70	(18)	56	a	56
Private	(303)	42	9	32	(289)	22	16	6
Two-year institutions								
Public	(314)	75	2	73	(308)	51	3	48
Private	(73)	34	7	27	(68)	38	4	34
Professional institutions								
Public	(15)	60	7	53	(14)	b	b	b
Private	(56)	43	4	39	(53)	36	2	34
Total	(1,137)	58	5	53	(1,101)	34	9	24
Graduate level programs								
Total	(426)	60	6	54	(430)	34	10	24
Professional level programs								
Total	(316)	47	2	46	(314)	36	3	32
Extension, evening, and/or continuing education programs								
Total	(727)	72	4	68	(728)	83	1	83

a No observations.

b Not calculated; base less than 15 cases.

Table 60. Percentages of institutions reporting increases in instructional programs at various program levels, by change in FTE enrollment, Carnegie type, and control, 1968–1974

| | | | | | Increase in programs | | | | |
Change in FTE enrollment	(N)	Under-graduate	(N)	Graduate	(N)	Profes-sional	(N)	Extension, evening, & continuing education
Research & doctoral universities								
Public:								
Increased enrollment	(46)	67	(46)	76	(40)	48	(46)	74
Little change, decreased	(19)	74	(18)	78	(15)	40	(17)	82
Private:								
Increased enrollment	(17)	47	(16)	50	(14)	a	(11)	a
Little change, decreased	(20)	25	(20)	10	(19)	21	(18)	33
Comprehensive colleges & universities								
Public:								
Increased enrollment	(115)	83	(98)	79	(51)	69	(103)	76
Little change	(27)	52	(22)	73	(11)	a	(20)	65
Decreased	(23)	57	(19)	42	(13)	a	(14)	a
Private:								
Increased enrollment	(32)	47	(24)	50	(15)	48	(23)	70
Little change	(24)	38	(18)	61	(14)	a	(19)	37
Decreased	(23)	48	(16)	69	(5)	a	(16)	44

Liberal arts, public & private								
Increased enrollment	(136)	60	(37)	51	(30)	60	(67)	69
Little change	(91)	44	(14)	a	(4)	a	(32)	59
Decreased	(82)	21	(9)	a	(5)	a	(38)	.68
Two-year institutions								
Public:								
Increased enrollment	(257)	81	(6)	a	(9)	a	(164)	92
Little change, decreased	(50)	46	(1)	a	(1)	a	(26)	69
Private:								
Increased enrollment	(25)	44	(1)	a	(2)	a	(11)	a
Little change, decreased	(40)	25	(1)	a	(3)	a	(17)	47
Professional schools, public & private								
Increased enrollment	(35)	51	(30)	47	(35)	43	(36)	64
Little change, decreased	(28)	39	(18)	39	(18)	28	(23)	57

a Not calculated; base less than 15 cases.

Note: "Increase" and "decrease" denote changes in enrollment of more than 10 percent. "Little change" denotes a change of up to ± 10 percent.

Table 61. Percentages of institutions reporting increases in instructional programs designed to serve "new students," actual 1968–1974 and anticipated 1974–1980, by change in number of instructional programs in extension, evening, continuing education programs, Carnegie type, and control, 1968–1974

| | Increase in number of instructional programs designed for | | | | | | | | | | | |
| | Ethnic minority | | | Adult over 22 | | | Evening | | | Off-campus | | |
Change in number of extension, evening & continuing ed. programs, 1968–1974	(N)	1968–1974	1974–1980	(N)	1968–1974	1974–1980	(N)	1968–1974	1974–1980	(N)	1968–1974	1974–1980
Universities & comprehensive colleges												
Public												
Increased	(147,146)	64	40	(148,147)	63	82	(145,144)	69	81	(138,139)	75	84
Little change or decreased	(53,51)	62	37	(52,51)	34	77	(52,53)	15	64	(45,46)	31	74
Private												
Increased	(41,40)	61	25	(44,41)	84	85	(42,39)	69	69	(37,36)	76	72
Little change or decreased	(44,44)	55	9	(40,42)	33	64	(41,41)	20	46	(29,30)	41	63

	(n, n)			(n, n)			(n, n)			(n, n)		
Liberal arts colleges												
Private												
Increased	(84,78)	44	32	(85,79)	75	94	(78,72)	80	86	(62,59)	69	86
Little change or decreased	(41,37)	39	19	(43,39)	23	80	(42,39)	14	69	(33,31)	24	65
Two-year institutions												
Public												
Increased	(162,156)	51	37	(165,161)	77	81	(170,163)	86	85	(159,154)	77	84
Little change or decreased	(22,22)	36	41	(22,22)	50	77	(22,22)	46	82	(21,21)	52	76

Table 62. Percentages of institutions reporting "extensive" change in emphasis on active recruitment of four types of students, by change in number of extension, evening, continuing education programs, Carnegie type, and control, 1968–1974

Change in number of extension, evening, continuing ed. programs	*Extensive change in active recruitment of four types of students*							
	(N)	*Ethnic minority*	*(N)*	*Adult over 22*	*(N)*	*Off-campus*	*(N)*	*Evening*
Universities & comprehensive colleges								
Public:								
Increased	(147)	66	(148)	33	(138)	34	(145)	36
Little change, decreased	(53)	69	(52)	19	(45)	22	(52)	24
Private:								
Increased	(41)	54	(44)	48	(37)	31	(42)	54
Little change, decreased	(44)	62	(40)	9	(29)	11	(41)	7
Liberal arts colleges								
Private:								
Increased	(84)	45	(85)	42	(62)	33	(78)	36
Little change, decreased	(41)	25	(43)	16	(33)	9	(42)	5
Two-year institutions								
Public:								
Increased	(162)	54	(165)	66	(159)	54	(170)	67
Little change, decreased	(22)	50	(22)	55	(21)	40	(22)	50

Table 63. Change in amount of funds for major functions, actual 1968–1974 and anticipated 1974–1980, by Carnegie type and control (in percentages of responding institutions)

Major function	(N)	1968–1974		(N)	1974–1980	
		In-creased	Little change		In-crease	Little change
Public						
Research universities						
Instruction & dept. res.	(36)	94	6	(34)	59	35
Sponsored research	(36)	75	14	(34)	53	41
Public service	(36)	64	31	(33)	52	46
Other doctoral						
Instruction & dept. res.	(33)	88	12	(32)	47	47
Sponsored research	(33)	64	24	(32)	44	53
Public service	(33)	67	33	(32)	56	44
Comprehensive colleges & universities						
Instruction & dept. res.	(168)	72	21	(166)	48	48
Sponsored research	(158)	42	49	(160)	36	56
Public service	(163)	47	47	(163)	46	51
Liberal arts colleges						
Instruction & dept. res.	(20)	75	25	(19)	68	32
Sponsored research	(16)	25	63	(16)	31	69
Public service	(18)	50	39	(18)	50	50
Two-year institutions						
Instruction & dept. res.	(324)	70	28	(317)	63	36
Sponsored research	(215)	21	75	(220)	20	76
Public service	(315)	69	29	(308)	65	34
Professional schools						
Instruction & dept. res.	(18)	72	28	(17)	71	29
Sponsored research	(16)	19	69	(16)	25	69
Public service	(17)	35	65	(17)	53	47
Private						
Research universities						
Instruction & dept. res.	(21)	81	14	(20)	55	45
Sponsored research	(21)	62	29	(20)	55	35
Public service	(20)	55	35	(19)	42	58
Other doctoral univ.						
Instruction & dept. res.	(19)	79	16	(19)	68	32
Sponsored research	(19)	42	21	(19)	42	53
Public service	(19)	26	63	(19)	21	79

Cont'd.

Table 63. Change in amount of funds for major functions, actual 1968–1974 and anticipated 1974–1980, by Carnegie type and control (in percentages of responding institutions) (Cont'd.)

	1968–1974				1974–1980	
Major function	*(N)*	*In-creased*	*Little change*	*(N)*	*In-crease*	*Little change*
Comprehensive colleges						
Instruction & dept. res.	(80)	70	25	(80)	58	43
Sponsored research	(75)	17	69	(76)	15	76
Public service	(77)	30	65	(78)	24	69
Liberal arts colleges						
Instruction & dept. res.	(308)	65	28	(298)	59	38
Sponsored research	(264)	15	71	(257)	14	77
Public service	(281)	28	67	(273)	30	63
Two-year institutions						
Instruction & dept. res.	(74)	55	37	(71)	59	41
Sponsored research	(40)	10	83	(39)	13	87
Public service	(53)	38	57	(52)	54	44
Professional schools						
Instruction & dept. res.	(86)	73	26	(84)	67	32
Sponsored research	(69)	16	75	(74)	30	66
Public service	(74)	30	66	(76)	34	65

Table 64. Percentages of institutions reporting anticipated "increase" in use of various teaching-learning modes as a result of changes in enrollment and/or funds 1974–1980, by change in FTE enrollment and in expenditures 1968–1974, Carnegie type, and control

					Increase in use of teaching-learning modes, 1974–1980		
Change in FTE enrollment and expenditures per FTE student, 1968–1974	(N)[a]	Lecture sections	Recitation/ discussion	Seminars	Labor- atory work	Self- study	Field work
Public universities & comprehensive colleges							
Increased enrollment and:							
Increased expenditures	(69)	33	23	36	25	81	80
Little change, decreased expenditures	(75)	16	15	23	22	83	80
Little change, decreased enrollment and:							
Increased expenditures	(23)	13	17	46	27	77	77
Little change, decreased expenditures	(37)	16	24	27	32	92	84
Private universities & comprehensive colleges							
Increased enrollment and:							
Increased expenditures	(23)	13	30	35	17	83	74
Little change, decreased expenditures	(20)	15	30	37	5	79	82
Little change, decreased enrollment and:							
Increased expenditures	(35)	17	27	49	26	82	71
Little change, decreased expenditures	(25)	8	8	28	12	72	67

Private liberal arts

Increased enrollment and:						
Increased expenditures	(55)	16	20	46	32	82	87
Little change, decreased expenditures	(45)	13	25	33	16	70	66
Little change and:						
Increased expenditures	(38)	b	11	49	37	84	92
Little change, decreased expenditures	(34)	15	21	35	15	77	79
Decreased enrollment and:						
Increased expenditures	(47)	11	19	46	26	78	89
Little change, decreased expenditures	(22)	9	32	73	33	91	100

Public two-year institutions

Increased enrollment and:						
Increased expenditures	(128)	16	28	50	39	87	71
Little change, decreased expenditures	(105)	14	26	40	40	90	76
Little change, decreased enrollment and:						
Increased expenditures	(20)	5	10	41	26	80	68
Little change, decreased expenditures	(24)	8	26	52	23	91	83

a The number of respondents applies to "Lecture Sections." Numbers upon which percentages are based for other teaching modes differ by at most 4 institutions among all types, except the public two year institutions: N varies from 0 to 17 fewer cases where enrollments increased and from 1 to 6 where both enrollment and expenditures did not change or decreased.

b No observations.

Note: "Increase" and "decrease" denote changes in enrollment and expenditures of more than 10 percent. "Little change" denotes a change of up to ± 10 percent.

Table 65. Change in financial support from various funding sources, actual 1968–1974 and anticipated 1974–1980, by Carnegie type and control (in percentages of responding institutions)

	1968–1974			1974–1980		
Funding sources	*(N)*	*More support*	*Little change*	*(N)*	*More support*	*Little change*
Public						
Research universities						
Local government	(11)	a	a	(11)	a	a
State government	(35)	94	6	(35)	77	20
Federal government	(36)	67	19	(36)	58	28
Endowment	(35)	54	46	(35)	51	43
Foundation & corp.	(35)	66	31	(35)	49	49
Private donors	(36)	72	25	(36)	61	33
Enrolled students	(36)	94	6	(36)	81	17
Continuing education	(36)	75	25	(36)	75	22
Doctoral universities						
Local government	(6)	a	a	(6)	a	a
State government	(33)	91	3	(32)	66	34
Federal government	(32)	63	22	(32)	41	50
Endowment	(24)	50	50	(24)	63	33
Foundation & corp.	(31)	58	42	(30)	57	43
Private donors	(31)	71	26	(29)	72	28
Enrolled students	(32)	81	13	(30)	63	37
Continuing education	(31)	65	35	(29)	76	24
Comprehensive colleges & universities						
Local government	(46)	28	67	(46)	30	67
State government	(170)	83	12	(166)	64	33
Federal government	(160)	59	29	(158)	42	46
Endowment	(93)	33	65	(95)	48	51
Foundation & corp.	(130)	45	52	(131)	51	44
Private donors	(145)	54	44	(147)	68	31
Enrolled students	(165)	77	18	(163)	61	36
Continuing education	(155)	61	36	(156)	70	28
Liberal arts colleges						
Local government	(5)	a	a	(5)	a	a
State government	(20)	85	15	(19)	79	21
Federal government	(19)	68	26	(19)	63	37
Endowment	(13)	a	a	(14)	a	a
Foundation & corp.	(18)	44	50	(18)	50	50
Private donors	(17)	53	35	(18)	61	39
Enrolled students	(19)	79	16	(19)	79	21
Continuing education	(16)	50	50	(16)	75	25

Table 65. Change in financial support from various funding sources, actual 1968–1974 and anticipated 1974–1980, by Carnegie type and control (in percentages of responding institutions) (Cont'd.)

Funding sources	(N)	1968–1974		(N)	1974–1980	
		More support	Little change		More support	Little change
Public (Cont'd.)						
Two-year colleges						
Local government	(258)	45	36	(254)	42	41
State government	(331)	78	17	(320)	74	23
Federal government	(319)	46	38	(309)	35	52
Endowment	(148)	16	83	(147)	30	66
Foundation & corp.	(197)	22	76	(199)	40	56
Private donors	(206)	24	73	(206)	43	54
Enrolled students	(301)	58	39	(298)	52	45
Continuing education	(293)	72	27	(287)	69	31
Professional colleges						
Local government	(7)	a	a	(5)	a	a
State government	(14)	a	a	(15)	73	27
Federal government	(16)	56	25	(17)	59	35
Endowment	(10)	a	a	(12)	a	a
Foundation & corp.	(12)	a	a	(14)	a	a
Private donors	(14)	a	a	(15)	60	40
Enrolled students	(14)	a	a	(14)	a	a
Continuing education	(13)	a	a	(13)	a	a
Private						
Research universities						
Local government	(8)	a	a	(7)	a	a
State government	(17)	82	18	(16)	63	38
Federal government	(21)	67	5	(19)	63	37
Endowment	(21)	67	24	(19)	79	16
Foundation & corp.	(21)	62	24	(19)	63	37
Private donors	(21)	81	14	(18)	83	17
Enrolled students	(21)	95	5	(19)	74	26
Continuing education	(21)	52	38	(19)	68	26
Doctoral universities						
Local government	(5)	a	a	(5)	a	a
State government	(12)	a	a	(12)	a	a
Federal government	(17)	35	35	(17)	59	29
Endowment	(19)	74	26	(18)	83	17
Foundation & corp.	(19)	63	32	(19)	63	37
Private donors	(19)	63	37	(17)	88	12
Enrolled students	(19)	68	26	(19)	68	26
Continuing education	(18)	33	61	(18)	72	28

Cont'd.

Table 65. Change in financial support from various funding sources, actual 1968–1974 and anticipated 1974–1980, by Carnegie type and control (in percentages of responding institutions) (Cont'd.)

Funding sources	(N)	1968–1974 More support	1968–1974 Little change	(N)	1974–1980 More support	1974–1980 Little change
Private (Cont'd.)						
Comprehensive colleges & universities						
Local government	(24)	21	75	(26)	15	85
State government	(60)	77	20	(57)	68	32
Federal government	(72)	40	39	(69)	48	46
Endowment	(82)	48	42	(79)	61	35
Foundation & corp.	(81)	59	35	(79)	65	34
Private donors	(82)	76	24	(79)	77	22
Enrolled students	(82)	82	11	(78)	65	27
Continuing education	(77)	47	47	(74)	62	37
Liberal arts colleges						
Local government	(89)	14	80	(89)	18	78
State government	(212)	75	24	(214)	69	28
Federal government	(273)	48	27	(265)	44	43
Endowment	(295)	51	41	(292)	76	22
Foundation & corp.	(302)	58	38	(296)	67	32
Private donors	(306)	77	20	(303)	87	13
Enrolled students	(310)	77	11	(307)	72	26
Continuing education	(243)	51	44	(236)	70	30
Two-year colleges						
Local government	(25)	8	88	(29)	21	79
State government	(44)	73	27	(48)	67	31
Federal government	(62)	65	27	(60)	58	33
Endowment	(58)	41	53	(60)	63	32
Foundation & corp.	(61)	51	46	(60)	65	33
Private donors	(69)	64	29	(65)	82	19
Enrolled students	(77)	66	22	(71)	66	32
Continuing education	(60)	43	53	(56)	70	30
Professional schools						
Local government	(22)	b	100	(22)	9	82
State government	(43)	61	37	(42)	71	26
Federal government	(54)	50	26	(54)	44	41
Endowment	(76)	49	46	(79)	68	27
Foundation & corp.	(77)	43	49	(77)	62	33
Private donors	(85)	65	32	(85)	85	13
Enrolled students	(87)	84	13	(86)	76	23
Continuing education	(68)	49	49	(70)	64	36

ª Not calculated; base less than 15 cases.

ᵇ No observations.

Table 66. Change in use of eight planning or management techniques, by Carnegie type and control, 1968–1974 (in percentages of responding institutions)

Planning/management techniques by Carnegie type	Public			Private		
	(N)	Exten- sive change	Very little change	*(N)*	Exten- sive change	Very little change
Research & doctoral universities						
Management information systems	(68)	34	6	(40)	35	17
Unit-cost studies	(68)	38	18	(39)	13	26
WICHE/NCHEMS products	(65)	25	35	(37)	5	57
Outside performance audits	(67)	7	54	(37)	11	54
Program evaluation	(67)	24	19	(37)	22	16
Analysis of institutional goals	(68)	31	19	(39)	33	8
Program budgeting/ management by objectives	(67)	22	34	(38)	10	55
Faculty workload studies	(68)	34	16	(38)	29	24
Comprehensive colleges & universities						
Management information systems	(164)	35	16	(79)	25	35
Unit-cost studies	(171)	27	21	(80)	29	20
WICHE/NCHEMS products	(160)	24	33	(68)	15	56
Outside performance audits	(159)	12	41	(71)	3	61
Program evaluation	(170)	22	20	(81)	23	20
Analysis of institutional goals	(171)	36	16	(82)	46	10
Program budgeting/ management by objectives	(166)	21	35	(76)	14	40
Faculty workload studies	(170)	38	9	(82)	26	18
Liberal arts institutions						
Management information systems	(18)	17	50	(280)	21	33
Unit-cost studies	(18)	6	44	(289)	15	31
WICHE/NCHEMS products	(18)	6	61	(239)	5	63
Outside performance audits	(17)	a	59	(265)	11	49
Program evaluation	(18)	11	44	(302)	30	14
Analysis of institutional goals	(18)	28	44	(301)	40	13
Program budgeting/ management by objectives	(18)	a	78	(282)	11	43
Faculty workload studies	(18)	6	28	(299)	17	20

Cont'd.

Table 66. Change in use of eight planning or management techniques, by Carnegie type and control, 1968–1974 (in percentages of responding institutions) (Cont'd.)

Planning/management techniques by Carnegie type	Public			Private		
	(N)	Exten- sive change	Very little change	(N)	Exten- sive change	Very little change
Two-year institutions						
Management information systems	(314)	24	23	(54)	18	41
Unit-cost studies	(318)	23	22	(61)	11	38
WICHE/NCHEMS products	(280)	15	43	(41)	2	68
Outside performance audits	(291)	10	49	(54)	17	52
Program evaluation	(321)	27	12	(69)	39	13
Analysis of institutional goals	(321)	30	12	(67)	39	10
Program budgeting/ management by objectives	(310)	22	28	(51)	23	37
Faculty workload studies	(325)	24	13	(64)	19	30
Professional schools						
Management information systems	(16)	25	19	(71)	17	39
Unit-cost studies	(16)	25	25	(75)	21	40
WICHE/NCHEMS products	(12)	b	b	(46)	6	83
Outside performance audits	(17)	18	29	(70)	13	40
Program evaluation	(17)	23	12	(82)	35	17
Analysis of institutional goals	(17)	35	12	(82)	39	10
Program budgeting/ management by objectives	(15)	27	13	(78)	14	44
Faculty workload studies	(17)	18	30	(82)	18	28

a No observations.

b Not calculated; base less than 15 cases.

Table 67. Change in FTE enrollment, by change in use of management information systems, Carnegie type, and control, 1968–1974 (in percentages of responding institutions)

Change in use of management information systems	(N)	Change in FTE enrollment		
		In-creased	Little change	De-creased
Universities & comprehensive colleges				
Public				
Extensive	(88)	75	22	3
Some	(109)	74	17	9
Very little	(28)	50	11	39
Private				
Extensive	(33)	49	24	27
Some	(48)	46	29	25
Very little	(34)	38	33	29
Private liberal arts colleges				
Extensive	(54)	43	35	22
Some	(124)	40	32	28
Very little	(89)	42	27	31
Public two-year institutions				
Extensive	(72)	90	4	6
Some	(161)	81	14	5
Very little	(73)	82	12	6

Note: "Increase" and "decrease" in enrollment denote changes of more than 10 percent. "Little change" denotes a change of up to ± 10 percent.

Table 68. Change in real operating expenditures, actual 1968–1974 and anticipated 1974–1980, by change in use of management information systems, Carnegie type, and control, 1968–1974

Change in use of management information systems	Change in expenditures per FTE student							
	1968–1974				1974–1980			
	(N)	In-creased	Little change	De-creased	(N)	In-crease	Little change	De-crease
Universities & comprehensive colleges								
Public								
Extensive	(86)	38	49	13	(81)	37	61	2
Some	(100)	47	46	7	(96)	30	65	5
Very little	(23)	57	39	4	(21)	33	62	5
Private								
Extensive	(29)	52	34	14	(28)	46	54	a
Some	(44)	64	34	2	(43)	61	37	2
Very little	(30)	53	47	a	(27)	41	59	a
Private liberal arts colleges								
Extensive	(57)	58	33	9	(54)	44	50	6
Some	(102)	59	38	3	(99)	50	46	4
Very little	(79)	58	39	3	(76)	43	54	3
Public two-year institutions								
Extensive	(69)	51	39	10	(67)	52	43	5
Some	(147)	55	40	5	(140)	55	42	3
Very little	(63)	53	41	6	(59)	49	48	3

[a]No observations.

Note: "Increase" and "decrease" denote changes in enrollment of more than 10 percent. "Little change" denotes a change of up to ±10 percent.

Table 69. Course and program consolidation or elimination in undergraduate, graduate, and professional levels, by change in use of management information systems, Carnegie type, and control 1968–1974 (in percentages of institutions reporting)

Change in use of management information systems	Course consolidation or elimination			Program consolidation or elimination		
	(N)	*Extensive or some in at least one level*	*All levels very little*	*(N)*	*Extensive or some in at least one level*	*All levels very little*
Universities & comprehensive colleges						
Public						
Extensive	(90)	44	56	(90)	41	59
Some	(105)	49	51	(105)	46	54
Very little	(29)	41	59	(29)	31	69
Private						
Extensive	(33)	67	33	(34)	47	53
Some	(49)	63	37	(49)	53	47
Very little	(34)	56	44	(34)	38	62
Private liberal arts colleges						
Extensive	(59)	56	44	(58)	48	52
Some	(123)	61	39	(118)	51	49
Very little	(90)	58	42	(88)	39	61
Public two-year institutions						
Extensive	(71)	48	52	(70)	53	47
Some	(146)	55	45	(148)	47	53
Very little	(68)	43	57	(67)	37	63

Table 70. Change in flexibility over campus use of state government funds, by change in use of management information systems, Carnegie type, and control, 1968–1974 (in percentages of responding institutions)

Change in use of management information systems	(N)	Flexibility over use of state funds		
		In-creased	Same	De-creased
Universities & comprehensive colleges				
Public				
Extensive change MIS	(90)	13	54	33
Some	(110)	7	52	41
Very little	(30)	13	40	47
Private				
Extensive change MIS	(28)	21	75	4
Some	(40)	12	88	a
Very little	(19)	a	84	16
Private liberal arts colleges				
Extensive change MIS	(43)	21	65	14
Some	(84)	10	83	7
Very little	(53)	13	74	13
Public two-year institutions				
Extensive change MIS	(75)	17	43	40
Some	(160)	13	66	21
Very little	(72)	11	70	19

[a]No observations.

Table 71. Change in use of management information systems (MIS), by extent of change in use of unit-cost studies, Carnegie type, and control, 1968–1974 (in percentages of responding institutions)

		Change in use of MIS		
Change in use of unit-cost studies	*(N)*	*Extensive*	*Some*	*Very little*
Universities & comprehensive colleges				
Public				
Extensive	(73)	71	28	1
Some	(113)	25	64	11
Very little	(46)	22	43	35
Private				
Extensive	(28)	57	29	14
Some	(65)	23	46	31
Very little	(24)	12	42	46
Private liberal arts colleges	(42)	64	26	10
Extensive	(144)	19	56	25
Some	(88)	7	36	57
Very little				
Public two-year institutions				
Extensive	(72)	58	31	11
Some	(167)	16	68	16
Very little	(69)	10	36	54

Table 72. Change in use of program evaluation, by change in use of
unit-cost studies, Carnegie type, and control, 1968–1974 (in
percentages of responding institutions)

Change in use of unit-cost studies	(N)	Change in use of program evaluation		
		Exten-sive	Some	Very little
Universities & comprehensive colleges				
Public				
Extensive	(73)	40	49	11
Some	(116)	16	63	21
Very little	(47)	13	57	30
Private				
Extensive	(27)	56	26	18
Some	(63)	16	73	11
Very little	(26)	4	57	39
Private liberal arts colleges				
Extensive	(44)	43	46	11
Some	(152)	31	62	7
Very little	(91)	23	46	31
Public two-year institutions				
Extensive	(73)	48	45	7
Some	(172)	23	65	12
Very little	(68)	13	68	19

Table 73. Extent of course and program consolidation or elimination in undergraduate, graduate, and professional levels, by change in use of unit-cost studies, Carnegie type, and control, 1968–1974 (in percentages of responding institutions)

Change in use of unit-cost studies	Course consolidation or elimination			Program consolidation or elimination		
	(N)	Extensive or some in at least one level	All levels very little	(N)	Extensive or some in at least one level	All levels very little
Universities & comprehensive colleges						
Public						
Extensive	(73)	52	48	(73)	47	53
Some	(113)	48	52	(114)	44	56
Very little	(45)	29	71	(44)	29	71
Private						
Extensive	(27)	70	30	(28)	36	64
Some	(65)	60	40	(65)	54	46
Very little	(25)	60	40	(25)	40	60
Private liberal arts colleges						
Extensive	(43)	67	33	(43)	51	49
Some	(147)	60	40	(139)	52	48
Very little	(89)	52	48	(88)	39	61
Public two-year institutions						
Extensive	(66)	53	47	(66)	54	46
Some	(158)	51	49	(156)	46	54
Very little	(65)	46	54	(65)	38	62

Table 74. Change in use of three selected planning/management techniques, by change in use of WICHE-NCHEMS products, Carnegie type, and control 1968–1974 (in percentages of responding institutions)

	Change in use of selected techniques								
	Management information systems			Unit-cost studies			Faculty workload studies		
Change in use of WICHE-NCHEMS products	(N)	Exten-sive	Very little	(N)	Exten-sive	Very little	(N)	Exten-sive	Very little
Universities & comprehensive colleges									
Public									
Extensive	(55)	69	a	(55)	73	4	(55)	67	a
Some	(93)	32	12	(95)	21	17	(94)	36	10
Very little	(73)	22	25	(74)	11	39	(75)	16	24
Private									
Extensive, some	(45)	49	9	(45)	38	7	(45)	44	7
Very little	(56)	14	50	(58)	14	31	(59)	14	32
Private liberal arts colleges									
Extensive, some	(85)	35	19	(87)	25	10	(89)	23	11
Very little	(146)	14	41	(147)	9	46	(150)	11	28
Public two-year institutions									
Extensive	(41)	66	5	(42)	74	5	(42)	57	12
Some	(117)	24	13	(117)	21	8	(118)	22	7
Very little	(119)	9	37	(116)	11	38	(120)	14	20

[a]No observations.

Table 75. Change in use of program evaluation, by change in use of WICHE-NCHEMS products, Carnegie type, and control, 1968–1974 (in percentages of responding institutions)

Change in use of WICHE-NCHEMS products	(N)	Change in use of program evaluation		
		Exten-sive	Some	Very little
Universities & comprehensive colleges				
Public				
Extensive	(55)	33	54	13
Some	(94)	20	62	18
Very little	(74)	15	54	31
Private				
Extensive, some	(43)	33	51	16
Very little	(59)	15	61	24
Private liberal arts colleges				
Extensive, some	(89)	36	55	9
Very little	(150)	25	56	19
Public two-year institutions				
Extensive	(42)	45	45	10
Some	(117)	34	57	9
Very little	(118)	14	68	18

Table 76. Anticipated change in use of WICHE-NCHEMS products
1974–1980, by actual change in use of WICHE-NCHEMS products
1968–1974, Carnegie type, and control (in percentages of
responding institutions)

Change in use of *WICHE-NCHEMS, 1968–1974*		Change in use of *WICHE-NCHEMS, 1974–1980*		
	(N)	Exten-sive	Some	Very little
Universities & comprehensive colleges				
Public				
Extensive	(55)	80	20	a
Some	(94)	48	51	1
Very little	(73)	33	48	19
Private				
Extensive, some	(45)	49	49	2
Very little	(53)	9	51	40
Private liberal arts colleges				
Extensive, some	(89)	31	64	5
Very little	(143)	6	42	52
Public two-year institutions				
Extensive	(42)	71	29	a
Some	(115)	43	56	1
Very little	(116)	24	41	35

[a] No observations.

Table 77. Change in use of management information systems (MIS) and unit-cost studies, by change in use of program performance audits by outside agencies, Carnegie type, and control, 1968–1974 (in percentages of responding institutions)

	Change in use of							
	MIS				*Unit-cost studies*			
Change in use of program performance audits	*(N)*	*Extensive*	*Some*	*Very little*	*(N)*	*Extensive*	*Some*	*Very little*
Universities & comprehensive colleges								
Public								
Extensive	(22)	64	27	9	(24)	46	29	25
Some	(96)	38	52	10	(100)	33	49	18
Very little	(101)	37	47	16	(101)	27	50	23
Private								
Extensive, some	(45)	29	56	15	(45)	22	67	11
Very little	(62)	24	36	40	(63)	25	43	32
Private liberal arts colleges								
Extensive	(27)	48	45	7	(29)	31	45	24
Some	(99)	18	50	32	(102)	14	57	29
Very little	(120)	17	43	40	(121)	16	47	37
Public two-year institutions								
Extensive	(29)	52	41	7	(29)	48	42	10
Some	(118)	27	61	12	(118)	26	59	15
Very little	(138)	16	48	36	(139)	15	55	30

Table 78. Change in use of four selected planning or management techniques, by USOE regions, Carnegie type, and control, 1968–1974 (in percentages of responding institutions)

Change in use of various management techniques	Management information systems				Unit-cost studies			
	North Atlantic	Grt. Lakes/ Plains	South-east	West/ Southwest	North Atlantic	Grt. Lakes/ Plains	South-east	West/ Southwest
Universities & comprehensive colleges								
Public	(N = 49)	(N = 60)	(N = 59)	(N = 64)	(N = 51)	(N = 60)	(N = 63)	(N = 65)
Extensive	47	38	41	31	29	16	27	20
Some	41	53	42	51	41	42	54	58
Very little	12	9	17	18	30	12	19	22
Private	(N = 56)	(N = 28)	(N = 11)	(N = 22)	(N = 57)	(N = 28)	(N = 11)	(N = 22)
Extensive	32	32	a	9	26	25	a	9
Some	41	43	a	50	53	61	a	55
Very little	27	25	a	41	21	14	a	36
Private liberal arts colleges	(N = 69)	(N = 105)	(N = 60)	(N = 46)	(N = 73)	(N = 105)	(N = 62)	(N = 49)
Extensive	22	20	23	22	12	18	13	16
Some	39	54	43	39	58	53	52	49
Very little	39	26	34	39	30	29	35	35
Public two-year institutions	(N = 55)	(N = 94)	(N = 53)	(N = 112)	(N = 55)	(N = 96)	(N = 53)	(N = 114)
Extensive	20	33	19	21	16	29	23	22
Some	54	52	55	51	55	53	53	57
Very little	26	15	26	28	29	18	24	21

Program performance audits
by outside agencies

WICHE-NCHEMS products

	WICHE-NCHEMS products				Program performance audits by outside agencies			
	North Atlantic	Grt. Lakes/ Plains	South-east	West/ Southwest	North Atlantic	Grt. Lakes/ Plains	South-east	West/ Southwest
Universities & comprehensive colleges								
Public	(N = 46)	(N = 58)	(N = 56)	(N = 65)	(N = 46)	(N = 58)	(N = 61)	(N = 61)
Extensive	35	28	18	20	11	14	6	11
Some	33	53	48	34	48	36	54	39
Very little	32	19	34	46	41	50	40	50
Private	(N = 51)	(N = 25)	(N = 9)	(N = 20)	(N = 52)	(N = 25)	(N = 10)	(N = 20)
Extensive, some	41	60	a	30	40	40	a	40
Very little	59	40	a	70	60	60	a	60
Private liberal arts colleges	(N = 62)	(N = 89)	(N = 47)	(N = 41)	(N = 66)	(N = 97)	(N = 58)	(N = 44)
Extensive, some	31	47	25	39	51	44	53	63
Very little	69	53	75	61	49	56	47	37
Public two-year institutions	(N = 50)	(N = 87)	(N = 45)	(N = 98)	(N = 50)	(N = 92)	(N = 46)	(N = 103)
Extensive	14	18	11	14	6	11	9	11
Some	40	47	35	42	38	51	35	37
Very little	36	35	54	44	56	38	56	52

a Not calculated; base less than 15 cases.

Note: *North Atlantic:* Connecticut, Delaware, District of Columbia, Maine, Maryland, Massachusetts, New Hampshire, New Jersey, New York, Pennsylvania, Rhode Island, Vermont
Great Lakes/Plains: Illinois, Indiana, Kansas, Michigan, Minnesota, Missouri, Nebraska, North Dakota, Ohio, South Dakota, Wisconsin
Southeast: Alabama, Arkansas, Florida, Georgia, Iowa, Kentucky, Louisiana, Mississippi, North Carolina, South Carolina, Tennessee, Virginia, West Virginia
West/Southwest: Alaska, Arizona, California, Colorado, Hawaii, Idaho, Montana, Nevada, New Mexico, Oklahoma, Oregon, Texas, Utah, Washington, Wyoming

Table 79. Shift in general decision-making authority from department to campus, actual 1968–1974 and anticipated 1974–1980, by Carnegie type and control (in percentages of responding institutions)

Carnegie type and control	1968–1974				1974–1980			
	(N)	Increased	Same	Decreased	(N)	Increase	Same	Decrease
Public								
Research & doctoral universities	(67)	25	56	19	(63)	35	59	6
Comprehensive	(167)	22	54	24	(162)	24	67	9
Liberal arts	(19)	32	68	a	(19)	16	68	16
Two-year	(305)	20	56	24	(292)	19	67	14
Professional	(15)	27	60	13	(14)	b	b	b
Private								
Research & doctoral universities	(38)	24	58	18	(35)	23	66	11
Comprehensive	(77)	26	48	26	(71)	28	68	4
Liberal arts	(277)	19	62	19	(248)	20	70	10
Two-year	(47)	21	64	15	(43)	19	65	16
Professional	(53)	23	62	15	(49)	25	65	10

a No observations.

b Not calculated; base less than 15 cases.

Table 80. Shift in general decision-making authority from governing board to various state offices reported by public senior colleges and universities,[a] actual 1968–1974 and anticipated 1974–1980, by change in authority from department to campus administration 1968–1974 (in percentages of responding institutions)

Shift in locus of general decision authority from department to campus administration, 1968–1974	1968–1974				1974–1980			
	(N)	Increased	Same	Decreased	(N)	Increase	Same	Decrease
From governing board to coordinating agency								
Increased campus administration	(37)	38	59	3	(37)	70	25	5
Same	(98)	47	50	3	(98)	59	41	b
Decreased	(36)	53	42	5	(36)	61	31	8
From governing board to state budget & finance (governor)								
Increased campus administration	(52)	71	27	2	(50)	62	32	6
Same	(118)	53	47	b	(118)	50	47	3
Decreased	(49)	31	63	6	(50)	37	59	4
From governing board to state legislature								
Increased campus administration	(50)	56	38	6	(51)	63	31	6
Same	(118)	35	63	2	(119)	43	55	2
Decreased	(50)	36	56	8	(51)	39	55	6

[a] Research universities, doctoral universities, and comprehensive colleges & universities.

[b] No observations.

Table 81. Shifts in general decision-making authority from governing board to various state offices reported by public senior colleges and universities,[a] by change in number of instructional programs designed to serve new students, 1968–1974 (in percentages of responding institutions)

	Shift in authority from governing board to					
	Coordinating agency		State budget & finance (governor)		State legislature	
Change in number of programs	Increased	Same, decreased	Increased	Same, decreased	Increased	Same, decreased
Programs for ethnic minorities	(N = 86)	(N = 94)	(N = 120)	(N = 116)	(N = 89)	(N = 142)
Increased	59	68	70	52	65	59
Little change, decreased	41	32	30	48	35	41
Programs for adults over 22 years	(N = 84)	(N = 94)	(N = 118)	(N = 113)	(N = 88)	(N = 141)
Increased	56	44	52	51	47	55
Little change, decreased	44	56	48	49	53	45
Programs for evening students	(N = 81)	(N = 91)	(N = 114)	(N = 109)	(N = 86)	(N = 135)
Increased	54	55	50	61	45	62
Little change, decreased	46	45	50	39	55	38
Programs for off-campus students	(N = 74)	(N = 82)	(N = 103)	(N = 104)	(N = 80)	(N = 128)
Increased	61	62	65	58	63	62
Little change, decreased	39	38	35	42	38	38

[a] Research universities, doctoral universities, comprehensive colleges and universities, and liberal arts colleges.

Table 82. Change in flexibility over campus use of state government funds reported by public institutions, by shift in general decision-making authority from governing boards to various state offices, 1968–1974 (in percentages of responding institutions)

Shift in authority from governing board to	(N)	Flexibility over use of state funds		
		In-creased	Same	De-creased
Coordinating agency				
Senior institutions[a]				
Increased	(87)	6	47	47
Same, decreased	(98)	14	54	32
Two-year institutions				
Increased	(75)	13	40	47
Same, decreased	(166)	15	65	20
State budget and finance (governor)				
Senior institutions[a]				
Increased	(121)	6	43	51
Same, decreased	(116)	15	54	31
Two-year institutions				
Increased	(114)	14	42	44
Same, decreased	(151)	14	72	15
State legislature				
Senior institutions[a]				
Increased	(90)	9	38	53
Same, decreased	(145)	11	55	34
Two-year institutions				
Increased	(105)	15	45	40
Same, decreased	(166)	13	68	19

[a]Research universities, doctoral universities, comprehensive colleges and universities, and liberal arts colleges.

Table 83. Change in use of various planning or management techniques reported by public institutions,[a] by shift in general decision-making authority from governing board to various state offices, 1968–1974 (in percentages of responding institutions)

Change in use of planning or management techniques	Shift in authority from governing board to					
	Coordinating agency		State budget & finance (governor)		State legislature	
	In-creased	Same, de-creased	Increased	Same, decreased	In-creased	Same, decreased
Management information						
systems	(N = 87)	(N = 93)	(N = 122)	(N = 113)	(N = 90)	(N = 141)
Extensive	45	32	32	37	33	40
Some	44	50	48	45	57	40
Very little	11	18	20	18	10	20
Unit-cost studies	(N = 89)	(N = 96)	(N = 122)	(N = 114)	(N = 91)	(N = 143)
Extensive	34	26	32	25	33	27
Some	52	53	48	54	51	50
Very little	14	21	20	21	16	23
Faculty workload						
studies	(N = 89)	(N = 96)	(N = 122)	(N = 113)	(N = 91)	(N = 142)
Extensive	36	37	37	34	41	32
Some	52	55	51	56	49	55
Very little	12	8	12	10	10	13
WICHE-NCHEMS						
products	(N = 84)	(N = 90)	(N = 115)	(N = 108)	(N = 89)	(N = 133)
Extensive	26	20	28	17	27	20
Some	41	40	38	46	42	42
Very little	33	40	34	37	31	38
Simulation	(N = 80)	(N = 86)	(N = 112)	(N = 105)	(N = 84)	(N = 131)
Extensive	5	5	7	2	6	5
Some	31	31	34	29	33	30
Very little	64	64	59	69	61	65

[a] Research universities, doctoral universities, comprehensive colleges and universities, and liberal arts colleges.

Table 84. Effect of institutional master plans on public senior colleges and universities,[a] by whether the institution is part of a system, 1968–1974 (in percentages of responding institutions)

Effect of institutional master plan, 1968–1974	*Institution part of a system*	*Institution not part of a system*
All institutions	(N = 120)	(N = 133)
Helped	71	64
No effect, hindered	14	11
No plan	15	25
Institutions with plans	(N = 102)	(N = 100)
Helped	83	85
No effect, hindered	17	15

[a] Research universities, doctoral universities, comprehensive universities and colleges, and liberal arts colleges.

Table 85. Change in FTE enrollment, actual 1968–1974 and anticipated 1974–1980, by reported effects of statewide master plans, 1968–1974 (in percentages of responding institutions)

| | Change in FTE enrollment | | | | | | | |
| | 1968–1974 | | | | 1974–1980 | | | |
Effect of statewide master plan, 1968–1974	(N)	Increased	Little change	Decreased	(N)	Increase	Little change	Decrease
Senior public institutions[a]								
Helped	(87)	77	16	7	(84)	45	50	5
No effect	(35)	69	14	19	(35)	31	66	3
Hindered	(40)	70	15	15	(39)	36	56	8
Senior private institutions[a]								
Helped	(56)	52	25	23	(76)	28	65	7
No effect	(97)	33	38	29	(54)	27	65	9
Hindered	(27)	30	19	52	(93)	22	67	11
Public two-year institutions								
Helped	(138)	89	9	2	(133)	62	38	1
No effect	(74)	81	15	4	(73)	49	44	7
Hindered	(36)	64	17	19	(34)	62	32	6

[a] Research universities, doctoral universities, comprehensive colleges and universities, and liberal arts colleges.

Note: "Increase" and "decrease" denote changes in enrollment of more than 10 percent. "Little change" denotes a change of up to ± 10 percent.

Table 86. Change in FTE enrollment, 1968–1974, by effect of
institutional master plan on institution 1968–1974 (in
percentages of responding institutions)

Effect of institutional master plan	(N)	Change in FTE enrollment		
		In-creased	Little change	De-creased
Senior public institutions[a]				
Helped	(163)	77	18	6
No effect, hindered	(31)	61	19	19
Senior private institutions[a]				
Helped	(266)	46	32	23
No effect, hindered	(56)	32	36	32
Public two-year institutions				
Helped	(251)	86	11	4
No effect, hindered	(32)	66	9	25

[a] Research universities, doctoral universities, comprehensive colleges and universities, and liberal arts colleges.

Note: "Increase" and "decrease" denote changes in enrollment of more than 10 percent. "Little change" denotes a change of up to ± 10 percent.

Table 87. Change in the use of management information systems, actual 1968–1974
and anticipated 1974–1980, by effect on institution of statewide master plan,
1968–1974 (in percentages of responding institutions)

	Change in use of management information systems							
	1968–1974				*1974–1980*			
Effect of statewide master plan, 1968–1974	*(N)*	*Exten-sive*	*Some*	*Very little*	*(N)*	*Exten-sive*	*Some*	*Very little*
Senior public institutions[a]								
Helped	(84)	41	50	9	(67)	79	18	4
No effect	(36)	17	56	28	(35)	49	49	3
Hindered	(42)	52	38	10	(30)	71	26	2
Senior private institutions[a]								
Helped	(58)	40	36	24	(58)	59	38	3
No effect	(93)	18	50	32	(89)	44	47	9
Hindered	(25)	16	48	36	(25)	56	28	16
Public two-year institutions								
Helped	(132)	28	56	16	(130)	72	27	1
No effect	(73)	22	51	27	(72)	43	49	8
Hindered	(35)	34	34	31	(35)	69	26	6

[a] Research universities, doctoral universities, comprehensive colleges and universities, and liberal
arts colleges.

Table 88. Shift in general decision-making authority from governing board to various state offices reported by public senior institutions[a], by USOE regions, 1968–1974 (in percentages of responding institutions)

Shift in authority from governing board to	USOE regions			
	North Atlantic	*Great Lakes/ Plains*	*South- east*	*West/ Southwest*
State coordinating agency	(N = 41)	(N = 42)	(N = 45)	(N = 59)
Increased	41	52	58	41
Same, decreased	59	48	42	59
State budget & finance				
(governor)	(N = 55)	(N = 60)	(N = 59)	(N = 65)
Increased	49	67	37	52
Same, decreased	51	33	63	48
State legislature	(N = 52)	(N = 60)	(N = 58)	(N = 67)
Increased	40	48	17	48
Same, decreased	60	52	83	52

[a] Research universities, doctoral universities, comprehensive colleges and universities, and liberal arts colleges.

Note: See Table 78 for a list of states in each region.

Table 89. Effect of statewide master plans on institutions, by USOE
region, 1968–1974 (in percentages of responding institutions)

Effect of statewide master plan	USOE regions			
	North Atlantic	Great Lakes/ Plains	South- east	West/ Southwest
Public senior institutions[a]	(N = 41)	(N = 41)	(N = 39)	(N = 47)
Helped	66	41	51	55
No effect	19	24	21	21
Hindered	15	35	28	24
Private senior institutions[a]	(N = 81)	(N = 58)	(N = 24)	(N = 25)
Helped	38	26	29	32
No effect	48	55	63	56
Hindered	14	19	8	12
Public two-year institutions	(N = 49)	(N = 72)	(N = 41)	(N = 90)
Helped	53	57	51	57
No effect	43	28	32	25
Hindered	4	15	17	18

[a] Research universities, doctoral universities, comprehensive colleges and universities, and liberal arts colleges.

Note: See Table 78 for a list of states in each region.

Table 90. Percentages of senior[a] and public two-year institutions reporting that statewide master plans helped their institutions, by selected states, 1968–1974

Institutions by state	State wide master plans	No plans	Plans either helped or hindered	Percentage of those with plans reporting helped	Ratio of helped to hindered
Twelve states with at least 15 institutions responding					
California	73	21	46	44	6.14
New York	69	c	51	68	11.75
Illinois	41	9	35	59	2.18
Pennsylvania	36	6	12	28	5.00[b]
Ohio	30	12	19	47	2.80
North Carolina	23	11	14	48	3.67[b]
New Jersey	20	3	11	40	2.67[b]
Texas	19	12	16	74	7.00
Minnesota	17	12	12	59	5.00[b]
Maryland	17	7	10	35	1.50[b]
Kansas	16	9	9	38	2.00[b]
Oklahoma	15	c	12	73	11.00[b]
Total	376	102	247	51	3.57
Nineteen states where half or more institutions report no plan	78	133	53	45	1.94
All other states	153	89	95	41	1.88
Total	607	324	395	48	2.76

Column headers (spanning): Number of institutions reporting: (State wide master plans, No plans, Plans either helped or hindered); Percentage of those with plans reporting helped; Ratio of helped to hindered.

[a] Research universities, doctoral universities, comprehensive colleges and universities, and liberal arts colleges.

[b] Ratio based on total smaller than 15.

[c] No observations.

Table 91. **Perceived effect of leveling of enrollment and funding on quality of students, programs, and faculty, by Carnegie type and control, 1974 (in percentages of responding institutions)**

Carnegie type and control	(N)[a]	Students		Programs		Faculty	
		Percent impairs	Ratio of impairs to enhances	Percent impairs	Ratio of impairs to enhances	Percent impairs	Ratio of impairs to enhances
Total	(941)	45	1.55	54	1.69	44	1.16
Public[b]							
Research	(26)	35	1.03	72	3.60	54	1.59
Other doctoral	(27)	44	1.47	65	2.83	67	2.58
Comprehensives	(137)	47	2.04	68	3.40	55	1.62
Two-year	(243)	34	.92	54	1.46	44	1.16
Total	(457)	39	1.22	(458) 59	1.97	(470) 48	1.30
Private							
Research	(18)	56	3.29	53	3.31	42	1.56
Other doctoral	(18)	44	2.59	44	1.33	50	1.79
Comprehensives	(72)	57	2.28	40	.89	33	.70
Liberal arts	(252)	51	1.89	50	1.52	43	1.19
Two-year	(60)	53	1.89	49	1.58	37	.86
Professional	(64)	34	1.00	51	1.96	33	.79
Total	(484)	50	1.85	(475) 48	1.45	(482) 40	1.03

[a] The number of respondents applies to students. In the case of programs and faculty, slightly different numbers of presidents responded.

[b] 13 public liberal arts colleges and 11 public professional schools not shown since base is less than 15 cases.

Table 92. Perceived effect of leveling of enrollment and funding on quality of students, programs and faculty, 1968–1974, by location, type, and control (in percentages of responding institutions)

Location of institutions	Students			Programs			Faculty		
	(N)	Enhances	Impairs	(N)	Enhances	Impairs	(N)	Enhances	Impairs
Universities									
Public:									
Large urban	(44)	25	43	(45)	24	62	(45)	40	49
Other urban	(24)	29	46	(23)	22	78	(24)	21	75
Small town, rural	(47)	17	43	(47)	19	64	(48)	29	54
Private:									
Large urban	(49)	27	47	(52)	33	48	(52)	29	48
Other urban & rural	(31)	13	43	(29)	21	38	(29)	31	24
Colleges (four-five year)									
Public:									
Large urban	(19)	21	42	(20)	15	80	(21)	24	67
Other urban	(24)	38	33	(23)	26	65	(25)	48	40
Small town, rural	(54)	30	54	(53)	28	59	(54)	44	46

Private:									
Large urban	(89)	29	49	(86)	34	51	(86)	41	42
Other urban	(116)	28	53	(110)	36	47	(114)	42	37
Small town, rural	(139)	27	48	(137)	33	50	(138)	36	43
Two-year institutions									
Public:									
Large urban	(48)	35	23	(48)	48	38	(49)	49	29
Other urban	(79)	39	35	(78)	41	54	(79)	37	48
Small town, rural	(115)	36	36	(118)	29	61	(121)	33	47
Private:									
Large urban	(21)	43	33	(20)	40	40	(21)	48	29
Other urban	(14)	a	a	(14)	a	a	(15)	47	7
Small town, rural	(25)	20	76	(26)	23	65	(26)	42	58

a Not calculated; base less than 15 cases.

Note: "Large urban" refers to "center of (downtown in) a large metropolitan area" and "elsewhere in an urban or metropolitan area"; "other urban" denotes "suburb of a large city" and "medium size city (50,000–100,000)"; and "small town, rural" includes the remaining category, "small town or rural area."

"Universities" include institutions offering a predoctorate or doctorate degree beyond the master's as the highest level of training. "Colleges" include institutions which offer a baccalaureate, a first-professional, or a master's degree as the highest level of training. "Two-year institutions" offer no more than an associate degree.

Table 93. Perceived effect of leveling of enrollment and funding on programs
and faculty, by effect on student quality, Carnegie type, and control,
1974 (in percentages of responding institutions)

Effect on student quality	Programs			Faculty		
	(N)	En-hances	Im-pairs	(N)	En-hances	Im-pairs
Universities and comprehensive colleges						
Public						
Enhances	(46)	54	41	(48)	60	35
Impairs	(84)	10	88	(85)	24	74
Neither	(47)	9	64	(48)	27	48
Private						
Enhances	(23)	74	9	(23)	78	9
Impairs	(58)	31	64	(58)	33	60
Neither	(21)	24	29	(21)	33	10
Private liberal arts colleges						
Enhances	(66)	77	17	(67)	72	21
Impairs	(119)	15	77	(125)	22	65
Neither	(41)	17	42	(40)	23	25
Public two-year institutions						
Enhances	(89)	67	32	(90)	64	32
Impairs	(80)	13	86	(81)	19	73
Neither	(51)	25	51	(52)	21	27

Table 94. Perceived effect of leveling of enrollment and funding on quality of students, programs, and faculty, by change in FTE enrollment and expenditures 1968–1974, Carnegie type, and control

Change in FTE enrollment and expenditures per FTE student	(N)[a]	Students		Programs		Faculty	
		Percent impairs	Ratio of impairs to enhances	Percent impairs	Ratio of impairs to enhances	Percent impairs	Ratio of impairs to enhances
Public universities & comprehensive colleges							
Increased enrollment and:							
Increased expenditures	(49)	33	1.14	53	1.83	48	1.20
Little change, decreased expenditures	(63)	54	2.25	76	4.22	54	1.38
Little change, decreased enrollment and:							
Increased expenditures	(20)	50	1.67	70	2.80	50	1.43
Little change, decreased expenditures	(36)	47	1.88	70	3.68	70	3.68
Private universities & comprehensive colleges							
Increased enrollment and:							
Increased expenditures	(20)	50	2.00	45	1.29	30	.60
Little change, decreased expenditures	(18)	67	3.05	44	1.00	33	.59
Little change, decreased enrollment and:							
Increased expenditures	(34)	50	2.08	46	1.35	40	1.08
Little change, decreased expenditures	(21)	57	4.07	38	1.00	52	3.71

Private liberal arts							
Increased enrollment and:							
Increased expenditures	(44)	46	1.28	40	.91	27	.51
Little change, decreased expenditures	(32)	41	1.08	42	1.59	33	.79
Little change enrollment and:							
Increased expenditures	(39)	44	1.69	50	1.56	46	1.28
Little change, decreased expenditures	(32)	50	2.27	45	1.18	42	1.31
Decreased enrollment and:							
Increased expenditures	(46)	65	3.82	62	2.00	59	2.57
Little change, decreased expenditures	(19)	63	5.73	56	2.55	53	2.04
Public two-year institutions							
Increased enrollment and:							
Increased expenditures	(100)	34	1.06	57	1.90	37	.97
Little change, decreased expenditures	(73)	38	1.06	47	1.04	47	1.31
Little change, decreased enrollment and:							
Increased expenditures	(16)	38	1.00	56	1.81	50	1.32
Little change, decreased expenditures	(23)	30	.63	52	1.33	57	2.19

ᵃ The number of respondents applies to students. See Table 95 for detailed table.

Note: "Increase" and "decrease" denote changes in enrollment and expenditures of more than 10 percent. "Little change" denotes a change of up to ± 10 percent.

Table 95. Perceived effect of leveling of enrollment and funding on quality of students, programs, and faculty, by change in FTE enrollment and in expenditures 1968–1974, Carnegie type, and control (in percentages of responding institutions)

Change in FTE enrollment and expenditures per FTE student, 1968–1974	Students			Programs			Faculty		
	(N)	Enhances	Neither	(N)	Enhances	Neither	(N)	Enhances	Neither
Public universities & comprehensive colleges									
Increased enrollment and:									
Increased expenditures	(49)	29	31	(49)	29	10	(50)	40	8
Little change, decreased expenditures	(63)	24	18	(62)	18	2	(65)	39	5
Little change, decreased enrollment &:									
Increased expenditures	(20)	30	15	(20)	25	a	(20)	35	10
Little change, decreased expenditures	(36)	25	28	(37)	19	8	(37)	19	11
Private universities & comprehensive colleges									
Increased enrollment and:									
Increased expenditures	(20)	25	15	(20)	35	5	(20)	50	10
Little change, decreased expenditures	(18)	22	11	(18)	44	6	(18)	56	6
Little change, decreased enrollment &:									
Increased expenditures	(34)	24	21	(35)	34	6	(35)	37	11
Little change, decreased expenditures	(21)	14	29	(21)	38	19	(21)	14	24

Private liberal arts colleges

Increased enrollment and:									
Increased expenditures	(44)	36	9	(45)	44	4	(45)	53	7
Little change, decreased expenditures	(32)	38	13	(33)	27	18	(33)	42	15
Little change enrollment &:									
Increased expenditures	(39)	26	28	(41)	32	16	(39)	36	15
Little change, decreased expenditures	(32)	22	25	(29)	38	14	(31)	32	19
Decreased enrollment and:									
Increased expenditures	(46)	17	13	(45)	31	4	(44)	23	16
Little change, decreased expenditures	(19)	11	21	(18)	22	11	(19)	26	11
Public two-year institutions									
Increased enrollment and:									
Increased expenditures	(100)	32	27	(102)	30	8	(103)	38	18
Little change, decreased expenditures	(73)	36	16	(71)	45	4	(75)	36	11
Little change, decreased enrollment &:									
Increased expenditures	(16)	38	12	(16)	31	6	(16)	38	a
Little change, decreased expenditures	(23)	48	13	(23)	39	4	(23)	26	13

a No observations.

Note: "Increase" and "decrease" denote changes in enrollment and expenditures of more than 10 percent. "Little change" denotes a change of up to ± 10 percent.

Table 96. **Modification of undergraduate admissions standards, by perceived effect of leveling enrollment and funding on student quality, change in FTE enrollment 1968–1974, Carnegie type, and control (in percentages of responding institutions)**

Change in FTE enrollment and effect on student quality[a]	Modification of undergraduate admissions standards	
	Extensive or some	Very little
Public senior institutions[b]		
Increased enrollment	(N = 43)	(N = 72)
Enhances student quality	23	30
Impairs	53	38
Neither	19	32
Little change or decreased enrollment	(N = 27)	(N = 34)
Enhances student quality	33	21
Impairs	56	47
Neither	11	32
Private senior institutions[b]		
Increased enrollment	(N = 40)	(N = 79)
Enhances student quality	20	46
Impairs	73	38
Neither	7	16
Little change or decreased enrollment	(N = 92)	(N = 112)
Enhances student quality	25	16
Impairs	64	54
Neither	12	30
Public two-year institutions		
Increased enrollment	(N = 71)	(N = 90)
Enhances student quality	45	31
Impairs	35	41
Neither	20	28

[a] Figures exclude the few institutions whose presidents responded "both" or "don't know."

[b] Research universities, doctoral universities, comprehensive colleges and universities, and liberal arts colleges.

Note: "Increase" and "decrease" denote changes in enrollment of more than 10 percent. "Little change" denotes a change of up to ± 10 percent.

Table 97. Modification of undergraduate admissions standards, by perceived effect of leveling enrollment and funding on student quality, change in expenditures 1968–1974, Carnegie type, and control (in percentages of responding institutions)

Change in expenditures per FTE student and effect on student quality[a]	*Modification of undergraduate admissions standards*	
	Extensive or some	*Very little*
Public senior institutions[b]		
Increased expenditures	(N = 38)	(N = 32)
Enhances student quality	32	38
Impairs	53	28
Neither	5	34
Little change or decreased expenditures	(N = 34)	(N = 66)
Enhances student quality	20	24
Impairs	65	50
Neither	15	26
Private senior institutions[b]		
Increased expenditures	(N = 74)	(N = 102)
Enhances student quality	24	30
Impairs	68	45
Neither	8	25
Little change or decreased expenditures	(N = 48)	(N = 71)
Enhances student quality	21	28
Impairs	65	49
Neither	14	23
Public two-year institutions		
Increased expenditures	(N = 47)	(N = 52)
Enhances student quality	45	27
Impairs	34	40
Neither	21	33

[a] Figures exclude the few institutions whose presidents responded "both" or "don't know."

[b] Research universities, doctoral universities, comprehensive colleges and universities, and liberal arts colleges.

Note: "Increase" and "decrease" denote changes in expenditures of more than 10 percent. "Steady" denotes a change of up to ± 10 percent.

Table 98. Change in emphasis on active recruitment of three types of students, by
perceived effect of leveling enrollment and funding on student quality, change
in FTE enrollment 1968–1974, Carnegie type, and control
(in percentages of responding institutions)

Change in FTE enrollment and effect on student quality[a]	Change in emphasis on active recruitment of					
	Early admits from high school		Adults over 22		Off-campus students	
	Extensive or some	Very little	Extensive or some	Very little	Extensive or some	Very little
Public senior institutions[b]						
Increased enrollment	(N=77)	(N=32)	(N=89)	(N=27)	(N=82)	(N=20)
Enhances student quality	22	44	25	33	28	25
Impairs	53	31	48	37	46	50
Neither	25	25	27	30	26	25
Little change or decreased enrollment	(N=34)	(N=26)	(N=49)	(N=13)	(N=44)	(N=13)
Enhances student quality	23	31	25	c	25	c
Impairs	56	42	53	c	50	c
Neither	21	27	22	c	25	c
Private senior institutions[b]						
Increased enrollment	(N=80)	(N=36)	(N=81)	(N=36)	(N=59)	(N=37)
Enhances student quality	40	28	38	28	42	32
Impairs	49	58	51	55	44	54
Neither	11	14	11	17	14	16
Little change or decreased enrollment	(N=139)	(N=59)	(N=126)	(N=69)	(N=99)	(N=55)
Enhances student quality	21	19	22	17	22	20
Impairs	57	61	60	55	62	56
Neither	22	20	18	28	16	24
Public two-year institutions						
Increased enrollment	(N=130)	(N=40)	(N=170)	(N=9)	(N=152)	(N=16)
Enhances student quality	38	38	38	c	42	19
Impairs	42	25	38	c	34	56
Neither	20	37	24	c	24	25

[a] Figures exclude the few institutions whose presidents responded "both" or "don't know."

[b] Research universities, doctoral universities, comprehensive colleges and universities, and liberal arts colleges.

[c] Not calculated; base less than 15 cases.

Note: "Increase" and "decrease" denote changes in enrollment of more than 10 percent. "Little change" denotes a change of up to ± 10 percent.

Table 99. Change in the number of undergraduate programs, 1968–1974, by perceived effect of leveling of enrollment and funding on student quality, change in FTE enrollment, selected Carnegie types,[a] and control (in percentages of responding institutions)

Change in FTE enrollment and effect on student quality[b]	Changes in number of programs for undergraduates	
	Increase	Little change or decrease
Public institutions with little change or decrease in enrollments, 1968–1974	(N = 36)	(N = 29)
Enhances student quality	28	24
Impairs	42	62
Neither	30	14
Private institutions with increased enrollments, 1968–1974	(N = 62)	(N = 56)
Enhances student quality	35	39
Impairs	55	45
Neither	10	16

[a] Research universities, doctoral universities, comprehensive colleges and universities, and liberal arts colleges.

[b] Figures exclude the few institutions whose presidents responded "both" or "don't know."

Note: "Increase" or "decrease" denote changes in enrollment of more than 10 percent. "Little change" denotes a change of up to ± 10 percent.

Table 100. Perceived effect of leveling enrollment and funding on student quality, by change in number of programs for "new students," 1968–1974, in public senior institutions reporting little change or a decrease in FTE enrollments, 1968–1974 (in percentages of responding institutions)

Change in number of programs in public senior institutions[a] *with little change or decrease in enrollments*		*Effect on student quality*		
	(N)	*Enhances*	*Impairs*	*Neither*
Programs for ethnic minorities				
Increased	(36)	28	47	25
Same or decreased	(28)	21	57	21
Programs for adults				
Increased	(29)	28	48	24
Same or decreased	(34)	20	56	24
Programs for evening students				
Increased	(31)	39	42	19
Same or decreased	(31)	13	58	29
Programs for off-campus students				
Increased	(33)	30	43	27
Same or decreased	(23)	17	61	22

[a] Research universities, doctoral universities, and comprehensive colleges and universities.

Note: "Increase" and "decrease" denote changes in enrollment of more than 10 percent. "Little change" denotes a change of up to ± 10 percent.

References

Bayer, A. E. *Teaching Faculty in Academe.* Washington, D.C.: American Council on Education, 1973.

Berdahl, R. O. *Statewide Coordination of Higher Education.* Washington, D.C.: American Council on Education, 1971.

Blackburn, R. T. *Tenure: Aspects of Job Security on the Changing Campus.* Atlanta: Southern Regional Education Board, July 1972.

Carnegie Commission on Higher Education. *The More Effective Use of Resources.* New York: McGraw-Hill, 1972.

Carnegie Commission on Higher Education. *A Classification of Institutions of Higher Education: A Technical Report.* Berkeley, Calif., 1973.

Center for Research and Development in Higher Education. *State Budgeting for Higher Education: Data Digest.* Berkeley, Calif.: University of California, 1975.

Cheit, E. F. *The New Depression in Higher Education.* New York: McGraw-Hill, 1971.

Cheit, E. F. *The New Depression in Higher Education—Two Years Later.* Berkeley, Calif.: Carnegie Commission on Higher Education, 1973.

Commission on Non-Traditional Study. *Diversity by Design.* San Francisco: Jossey-Bass, 1973.

Cross, K. P. *Beyond the Open Door: New Students to Higher Education.* San Francisco: Jossey-Bass, 1971.

Glenny, L. "The Illusions of Steady State." *Change Magazine,* Winter 1974–75, *6* (10).

Glenny, L. A., Berdahl, R., Palola, E., and Paltridge, G. *Coordinating Higher Education for the '70s.* Berkeley, Calif.: Center for Research and Development in Higher Education, University of California, 1971.

Glenny, L., and Kidder, J. *State Tax Support of Higher Education: Revenue Appropriation Trends and Patterns 1963–1973.* Report no. 47. Denver, Colo.: Education Commission of the States, April 1974.

Heilbroner, R. L. *An Inquiry into the Human Prospect.* New York: W. W. Norton, 1974.

Huckfeldt, V. *Change in Higher Education Management.* Boulder, Colo.: NCHEMS at WICHE, 1972.

Jencks, C., and Riesman, D. *The Academic Revolution*. New York: Double-day, 1968.

Kerr, C. *Uses of the University*. Cambridge, Mass.: Harvard University Press, 1964.

Lee, E. C., and Bowen, M. *Managing Multicampus Systems: Effective Administration in an Unsteady State*. San Francisco: Jossey-Bass, 1975.

Leslie, L. L., and Miller, H. F., Jr. *Higher Education and the Steady State*. ERIC/Higher Education Research Report No. 4. Washington, D.C.: American Association for Higher Education, 1974.

Mann, W. R. "Is the Tenure Controversy a Red Herring?" *Journal of Higher Education*, February 1973, *44*, 85–94.

Medsker, L., et al. *Extending Opportunities for a College Degree: Practices, Problems, and Potentials*. Berkeley, Calif.: Center for Research and Development in Higher Education, University of California, 1975.

U.S. Bureau of the Census. "Population Characteristics." *Current Population Reports*, ser. P-20, no. 260, Washington, D.C., February 1974.

U.S. National Center for Educational Statistics. *Education Directory 1973–74: Higher Education*. Washington, D.C., 1974.

Veysey, L. "Stability and Experiment in the American Undergraduate Curriculum." In C. Kaysen (Ed.), *Content and Context*. New York: McGraw-Hill, 1973.

Wilms, W. W. "A New Look at Proprietary Schools." *Change Magazine*, Summer 1973, *5* (6), 6.

Index

A

Administration: campus, authority shifts and, 75, 76–78, 228; size of, 33, 35; for student recruitment, 35, 46

Admissions: early, 45, 48; open, 11, 16, 148–149; modified, 47–48, 92, 191, 192, 250

Agriculture, enrollment in, 21, 25

Architecture, enrollment in, 25

B

BAYER, A. E., 34, 255

BERDAHL, R. O., 85, 255

Biological sciences, enrollment in, 21, 23, 25

BLACKBURN, R. T., 34, 255

BOWEN, F., 74n, 256

Building program, in steady state conditions, 17–18, 152–155

Business, enrollment in, 21, 23, 24, 25, 26

C

California, 72, 82, 83

Carnegie Commission on Higher Education, 3, 16, 255

Center for Research and Development in Higher Education, 78n; State Budgeting Study by, 40, 55, 70, 255

CHEIT, E. F., 1, 255

Closure, of institutions, 57, 58–59

Collective bargaining, 40–42, 104

College and University Systems Exchange (CAUSE), 61

Comprehensive institutions: authority shifts and, 76; curriculum in, 23, 25; expenditures per student by, 16; faculty at, 37; impact of enrollment leveling on, 91; management techniques used by, 63, 66–67, 68, 71

Comprehensive institutions, private: curriculum in, 30; enrollment trends in, 10, 11; expenditures per student by, 15; faculty at, 35, 36, 38, 41; impact of enrollment leveling on, 89; management techniques at, 70; program changes at, 49, 50

Comprehensive institutions, public: authority shifts and, 77–80, 82–83; enrollment trends in, 9, 10, 11, 13; expenditures per student by, 15; faculty at, 35, 36, 38, 40, 41; impact of enrollment leveling on, 88, 90; management techniques at, 70; reorganization of, 57

Coordinating agency, authority shifts and, 75, 78–79, 80, 83–84

Courses, consolidation of, 29–30, 64, 68, 106–107, 217, 221

CROSS, K. P., 28n, 255

Curriculum: enrollment related to,